DRAMA CLAS

The Drama Classics ser

plays in affordable paperback editions for students, actors and theatregoers. The hallmarks of the series are accessible introductions, uncluttered texts and an overall theatrical perspective.

Given that readers may be encountering a particular play for the first time, the introduction seeks to fill in the theatrical/historical background and to outline the chief themes rather than concentrate on interpretational and textual analysis. Similarly the play-texts themselves are free of footnotes and other interpolations: instead there is an end-glossary of 'difficult' words and phrases.

The texts of the English-language plays in the series have been prepared taking full account of all existing scholarship. The foreign-language plays have been newly translated into a modern English that is both actable and accurate: many of the translators regularly have their work staged professionally.

Edited until his early death by Kenneth McLeish, the Drama Classics series continues with his aim of providing a first-class library of dramatic literature representing the best of world theatre.

Associate editors:
Professor Trevor R. Griffiths
Professor in Humanities, University of Exeter
Dr Colin Counsell
Senior Lecturer in Theatre Studies and Performing Arts

Drama Classics *the first hundred*

The Alchemist
All for Love
Andromache
Antigone
Bacchae
Bartholomew Fair
The Beaux Stratagem
The Beggar's Opera
Birds
Blood Wedding
The Changeling
A Chaste Maid in
    Cheapside
The Cherry Orchard
Children of the Sun
El Cid
The Country Wife
The Dance of Death
The Devil is an Ass
Doctor Faustus
A Doll's House
Don Juan
The Duchess of Malfi
Edward II
Electra (Euripides)
Electra (Sophocles)
An Enemy of the
    People
Everyman
The Father
Faust
A Flea in her Ear
Frogs
Fuente Ovejuna
The Game of Love
    and Chance
Ghosts
The Government
    Inspector
Hecuba
Hedda Gabler
The House of
    Bernarda Alba

The Hypochondriac
The Importance of
    Being Earnest
An Ideal Husband
An Italian Straw Hat
Ivanov
The Jew of Malta
The Knight of the
    Burning Pestle
The Lady from the
    Sea
The Learned Ladies
Lady Windermere's
    Fan
Life is a Dream
London Assurance
Lulu
Lysistrata
The Malcontent
The Man of Mode
The Marriage of
    Figaro
Mary Stuart
The Master Builder
Medea
The Misanthrope
The Miser
Miss Julie
A Month in the
    Country
Oedipus
The Oresteia
Peer Gynt
Phedra
The Playboy of the
    Western World
The Recruiting Officer
The Revenger's
    Tragedy
The Rivals
La Ronde
Rosmersholm
The Rover

Scapino
The School for
    Scandal
The Seagull
The Servant of Two
    Masters
She Stoops to Conquer
The Shoemakers'
    Holiday
Six Characters in
    Search of an
    Author
The Spanish Tragedy
Spring Awakening
Summerfolk
Tartuffe
Three Sisters
'Tis Pity She's a
    Whore
Too Clever by Half
Ubu
Uncle Vanya
Volpone
The Way of the World
The White Devil
The Widowing of Mrs
    Holroyd
The Wild Duck
A Woman Killed with
    Kindness
A Woman of No
    Importance
Women Beware
    Women
Women of Troy
Woyzeck
Yerma

*The publishers welcome
suggestions for further titles*

DRAMA CLASSICS

FUENTE OVEJUNA

by

Lope de Vega

translated by Laurence Boswell
introduced by William Gregory

NICK HERN BOOKS

London

www.nickhernbooks.co.uk

A Drama Classic

Fuente Ovejuna first published in Great Britain in this translation as a paperback original in 2009 by Nick Hern Books Limited, The Glasshouse, 49a Goldhawk Road, London W12 8QP

Reprinted 2014

Typeset by Country Setting, Kingsdown, Kent CT14 8ES
Printed and bound in Great Britain by Mimeo Ltd, Huntingdon, Cambridgeshire PE29 6XX

A CIP catalogue record for this book is available from the British Library

ISBN 978 1 84842 023 6

Introduction

Félix Lope de Vega y Carpio (1562–1635)

Nicknamed 'a monster of nature' and 'the phoenix of Spain', Lope de Vega was astonishing in his dramatic output. He has been praised as the most popular poet, in both senses, in Spanish history, and is credited by some with having the most abundant vocabulary of any writer in the world. Claiming in his own words to have penned over 1,500 plays, and at a frantic pace, Lope left behind over 400 examples of his work, although not all of these can be attributed to him with complete certainty.

For a man who would go on to become Spain's most famous and prolific playwright, the place and time of Lope de Vega's birth could hardly have been more auspicious. Born just two years before Marlowe, Shakespeare and Galileo, and counting such Spanish literary and artistic giants as writer Miguel de Cervantes, painter Diego Velázquez and poets Luis de Góngora and Francisco de Quevedo among his contemporaries, Lope was born in Madrid on 25 November 1562, just one year after Philip II had made the city the capital of Spain, and when the country was in its ascendancy: it was Spain's 'Golden Age', with the Low Countries, Genoa, parts of North Africa and all of modern-day Spain under Philip II's control, Portugal to be annexed a few years later, trade flourishing with the Americas and the population booming.

The son of master embroiderer Félix de Vega Carpio
and Francisca Fernández Flores, from the north of Spain,
Lope grew up in Madrid's bustling Puerta de Guadalajara
district. Proud of their city's new royal status and revelling
in any opportunity to celebrate it, the people of Madrid
lived a raucous street-life, with merchants selling everything
from toiletries to hot snacks on the busy city's broad central
avenues and winding lanes, and cries of '¡Agua va!' ('Water
ho!') coming from the upper windows, announcing the
emptying of chamber pots in the absence of privvies. Meanwhile, the gardens of the Prado, where ladies rode around in
their carriages, were a haven of calm for high society, and at
the Manzanares River housemaids struggled to do the
laundry despite it often having little or no water.

If the accounts of some of his earlier biographers are to be
believed, Lope was a precocious child, who could read both
Latin and Spanish by the time he was five and began
composing verses before he could even write. Having
studied at a Jesuit college as a youngster, Lope went up to
the prestigious University of Alcalá de Henares (some 35 km
from Madrid), where he gained a great deal of experience, if
not a degree. According to his own writings (on which so
much of the playwright's life story is based, but which may
be peppered with exaggeration), Lope left university early,
blinded by his love for a woman. A brief spell at the
University of Salamanca followed, until in 1583 he joined a
military expedition to Terceira, an island in the Azores and
the only Portuguese territory yet to be annexed by the
Spanish Crown; he returned victorious. By now, and still
only in his early twenties, Lope was already a well-established
poet, and in 1585 was praised for his precociousness by
none other than literary colossus Miguel de Cervantes.

Lope was once described as a man who 'lived literature and made literature from life', and his eventful biography lives up to the claim. By 1588, Lope was a successful playwright, accepting commissions from companies in Madrid's ever-growing theatrical scene. One such theatre company was owned by Jerónimo Velázquez. Lope had entered into a tempestuous affair with Velázquez's married daughter, Elena Osorio, although it seems the girl's father turned a blind eye in exchange for the fruits of Lope's writing prowess. When the affair ended and a number of libellous poems began to appear around Madrid, with Velázquez and his family as their subject matter, the director was less tolerant, however. Lope denied any involvement, but was put on trial for the poetry and sentenced to eight years of exile from the court of Madrid, and two years from the realm of Castile, the heartland of Spain.

Having broken his exile in order to abduct and marry his first wife, Isabel de Alderete y Urbina, in May 1588 (it seems she was a willing victim), Lope went to Lisbon just nineteen days later to enlist with the Spanish Armada. The playwright joined the crew of the San Juan on the famous fleet's fateful attempt to attack Elizabeth I's England. Lope's brother, Juan, died at sea that year, but Lope lived to tell the tale, and to go on writing. Still exiled from Madrid, Lope moved to Valencia in 1589, and continued to ply his ever-more-successful trade as a playwright in the Mediterranean city. Valencia was an important centre for literature and printing, and with many of his poems and songs being published, Lope was by 1590 somewhat of a national star. Not yet thirty, Lope was by now the most popular playwright in Madrid, despite still being forbidden from coming within five leagues of the city.

In 1590, Lope moved to Toledo to take a position as secretary to Antonio, Duke of Alba, but in 1595, following the death that year of his wife, who had born him two children, the playwright returned to Madrid, his period of banishment cut short. In 1598, Lope's second marriage to Juana de Guardo, the daughter of a wealthy butcher, coincided with a ban on theatre imposed by Philip II, in mourning for the death of his daughter. That same year, however, Philip II also died, and was succeeded by his less serious son, Philip III. The new king married Margaret of Austria in 1599, and Lope was commissioned to write a number of new plays for the celebrations, which took place in Valencia. Appointed as secretary from 1598 to 1600 to Pedro Fernández de Castro, Lope's theatrical repertoire now numbered over one hundred texts.

Though still married to Juana de Guardo, with whom he had three children, Lope now embarked on an affair with Micaela de Luján, an actress and mother of two whose actor-husband had lived in Peru since 1596 and died in 1603. In 1604, Micaela gave up acting and became a tutor to Lope's children; she bore him two further offspring, and until 1610 the playwright divided his life between Juana and Micaela in Toledo and Madrid, before settling, for the time being, in the capital. During these early years of the seventeenth century, Lope was at his peak as a writer, and in his Madrid home he wrote some of his most famous plays, including *El perro del hortelano* (*The Dog in the Manger*), *La dama boba* (*The Foolish Woman*), *El caballero de Olmedo* (*The Knight of Olmedo*), *Peribáñez* and *Fuente Ovejuna*, and in 1609, he published a treatise on playwriting, *El arte nuevo de hacer comedias* (*The New Art of Playwriting*). In 1613, however, events took a turn for the worse, and Lope's life once again took a dramatic twist. The playwright's son, Carlos Félix, died, and shortly afterwards, so did Juana de Guardo.

One year later, aged 52, Lope moved again to Toledo and joined the priesthood; there followed five years of increasing dedication to the Church, but Lope continued his involvement with the theatre and, it seems, with women. Another affair ensued, this time with one Marta de Nevares Santoyo, a 26-year-old whose tender age, compared with Lope's, invited mockery from such famed contemporaries as Góngora. This passionate affair, which seems to have inspired Lope to write prolifically in his later years, was almost scuppered when Marta was forced into marriage and dragged off to Valladolid, until the groom unexpectedly died. Lope became a friar in 1627, was awarded an honorary doctorate in theology, and even received the Saint John's Cross from the Pope.

In 1635, ailing and following the death of another son, Lope began to wish for his life to end. His death on 27 August 1635 was marked by a nine-day funeral in which all of Madrid was involved. It was paid for by the Duke of Sessa, to whom Lope had been secretary since 1605. By the time of his death, Lope's fame and prestige was such that, as the priest presiding over the funeral said, 'de Lope' ('of Lope') had become a byword for all that was of the highest quality.

Fuente Ovejuna: **What Happens in the Play**

The play opens in the spring of 1476 in Almagro, in the medieval kingdom of Castile. At the residence of the Holy Order of the Knights of Calatrava, Fernán Gómez de Guzmán, the Chief Commander of the Order, reports to its

Grand Master, Rodrigo Téllez Girón. The throne of Castile is at stake following the death of Enrique IV: King Ferdinand of Aragon claims the Crown through his marriage to Enrique's sister, Isabella; Téllez Girón, however, supports Alfonso V of Portugal, whose wife is Enrique's only natural child. Guzmán urges the Grand Master to capture the strategic town of Ciudad Real; Téllez Girón agrees.

Meanwhile, in Fuente Ovejuna (literally, 'Sheep-Well'), the humble town where Guzmán is stationed and over which he has authority, local peasant girl Laurencia rails against the Commander to her friend, Pascuala: Guzmán has been attempting to seduce her. The Commander and his men arrive, victorious after capturing Ciudad Real, and the locals of Fuente Ovejuna lavish tributes upon him. Guzmán makes another, failed attempt to use his high status to 'persuade' Laurencia into a liaison.

The action then moves to Toledo, the city from which the revered Catholic Monarchs Ferdinand and Isabella rule Castile and Aragon. When they hear of Téllez Girón's treacherous capture of Ciudad Real, they resolve to retake the city.

Back in Fuente Ovejuna, a flirtation between Laurencia and her peasant-sweetheart Frondoso is interrupted by Guzmán. Failing again to talk Laurencia into sex, the Commander decides to take her by force, placing his crossbow on the ground as he advances. Frondoso picks up the weapon to defend Laurencia's honour; he and the girl flee, keeping the crossbow for protection.

Act Two begins badly for Guzmán: Laurencia's father, Esteban, Mayor of Fuente Ovejuna, defends his daughter's defiance despite his own lowly rank; Frondoso is still at large; and news arrives that the Catholic Monarchs have retaken Ciudad Real. Guzmán and his knights hasten to Téllez Girón's aid. They kidnap a local girl, Jacinta, taking her off to battle with them, and beat peasant lad Mengo black and blue for trying to defend her.

In Ciudad Real, Guzmán and Téllez Girón's men are overwhelmed by the Catholic Monarchs'. While they are away, Frondoso proposes marriage to Laurencia. On their return to Fuente Ovejuna, the furious Commander and his men break up the wedding party: they arrest the groom, beat Esteban, tie Laurencia up and drag her away.

By Act Three, the townspeople are tiring of such outrages. Ferdinand and Isabella's troops are on their way, but what to do in the meantime? Evacuate? Continue suffering? Or fight back? Their minds are made up by the arrival of Laurencia: dishevelled, transfigured, desperate, she has, it seems, been raped. The peasants amass at Guzmán's residence, forcing him to release Frondoso. The mob bays for Guzmán to be hurled from the window and impaled on their spears.

Later, with Guzmán's head displayed upon a spike, the villagers revel in their victory, but worry that the arrival of the Catholic Monarchs' forces will mean an investigation into the murder of the Commander, technically their master and one to whom they owe allegiance. They resolve to say only that 'Fuente Ovejuna did it' when questioned. A judge does indeed arrive, and the investigation begins, but the folk of Fuente Ovejuna stay true to their word: Esteban, Pascuala, Mengo and even a small boy, despite being tortured on the rack, confess only that 'Fuente Ovejuna did it.'

The play ends at the Catholic Monarchs' court in Córdoba, where a repentant Téllez Girón is brought back into the fold. The judge tells Ferdinand and Isabella that his investigation in Fuente Ovejuna has failed. He has brought almost the entire town with him, either to be executed en masse, or to be pardoned. Hearing of the outrages suffered by the peasants, King Ferdinand grants them forgiveness.

Fuente Ovejuna: **Themes and Contexts**

Spain was still revelling in its ascendancy at the time of Lope's birth, but by the time he wrote *Fuente Ovejuna*, around the second decade of the seventeenth century, things had changed. Demographic expansion in Spain began to slow from 1580; economic crises threatened food supplies between 1605 and 1607, and 1615 and 1616; industry began to decline; the rich-poor divide grew; and an increasing number of Spaniards left the country to seek a better life overseas. Spain's military pride had been dented by the defeat of the Armada at the hands of the English navy in 1588, and Philip II's undiminished military spending left his successor, Philip III, with enormous debts to resolve. An Anglo-Spanish peace accord was signed in 1604 following the death of Elizabeth I, and 1609 saw the beginning of a twelve-year truce with Antwerp following the failure of a 1605–6 offensive against Dutch rebels.

Golden Age

Fuente Ovejuna arose in this context of slowly diminishing Spanish confidence, but also as part of a steep upward trajectory of Spanish literature and scholarship. Some twenty-two new universities opened in Spain in the sixteenth century, with literacy rates rising in the Iberian Peninsula with the increasing availability of printed books. The first ever grammar of the Spanish language had appeared in 1492, and by around 1550 the Golden Age had truly begun, with the anonymous picaresque novel *Lazarillo de Tormes* being written in 1554. The Spanish literary giant Miguel de Cervantes was born in 1547, writing the first volume of one of Spain's most important literary works, *Don Quijote de la Mancha (Don Quixote)*, in 1605.

Theatre had been developing, too, having begun in the Middle Ages with religious dramas performed in churches. Spain's theatrical output in the sixteenth and seventeenth centuries was said to exceed that of all the rest of Europe combined. Born around 1485, playwright Bartolomé de Torres Naharro became the first Spaniard to write plays in the style adopted later by Lope de Vega, and was recognised by Lope himself as one of the forefathers of Spanish playwriting, along with the more famous Lope de Rueda. Born around 1510 in Seville, actor-dramatist Lope de Rueda laid the foundations for what would become Golden Age drama, touring Spain's courtyards, squares and palaces with his comic plays, or *pasos*, combining elements of Spanish comedy with those of popular Italian dramas. By the time he wrote *Fuente Ovejuna*, Lope de Vega had secured his own place in this theatrical hall of fame.

As just one text plucked from Lope's huge oeuvre, *Fuente Ovejuna* shares many typical traits with its fellow Golden Age plays. Based on historical events, the play combines high drama with elements of humour, philosophical musings such as those on the nature of love and the urban-rural divide, a celebration of the legendary Catholic Monarchs, heroes and villains, singing and dancing, romance and violence, and a happy ending. It is fare that the boisterous audiences of the *corrales*, Madrid's theatres, would have relished. *Fuente Ovejuna* stands out, however, not only as a fine example of its genre, but also as one that breaks the mould.

Collective Action

The most salient and unusual feature of *Fuente Ovejuna* is the collective action of the humble townspeople in overthrowing and killing the tyrant Guzmán. Despite commanding the respect due to his rank, the Commander is defeated by a popular uprising, with the entire town taking up often makeshift arms and executing Guzmán even as he is about to commit an execution of his own. Writing in the early twentieth century, Spanish scholar Marcelino Menéndez y Pelayo remarked that there was 'no play more democratic' in Spanish-language theatre, and the idea of 'the people' as *Fuente Ovejuna*'s true protagonist was one seized upon by many modern practitioners, not least those on the political left.

True, political theory books at the time of *Fuente Ovejuna*'s writing were beginning to call for more equal treatment between master and subject, and the military orders, represented by Téllez Girón and Guzmán, were by the seventeenth century losing their social prestige. The reading of *Fuente Ovejuna* as a celebration of 'people power' and, by extension, as a challenge to the orthodoxy of both the fifteenth century, when the play is set, and of the seventeenth, when it was written, may, however, be altogether too modern. Alongside the collective claim of 'Fuente Ovejuna did it' comes the chant, equally heart-felt, of 'Long live the Catholic Monarchs', and here lies the true meaning of the plucky townspeople's revolt. The rebellion against Guzmán is a rebellion not against social hierarchy, but against a tyrant, not to mention a traitor. The collective action of the townsfolk does not challenge the supremacy of the ruling classes; it restores it, and is bound up with the ubiquitous Golden Age theme of honour.

Honour

Whilst the importance of honour in everyday life in the Spanish Golden Age may be open to debate, its position as a focus for literature in the period is central. Manifesting itself in many forms, honour in the Golden Age tradition is essentially a notion of respect, owed, earned and lost. Honour is a measure of the respect due to those of high rank, and to those of virtue. It is shown to those of noble standing by obedience to formal etiquette and the offering of tributes, but also to those of lower rank, by those higher up the scale behaving according to social norms. Honour is also personal, and sexual. A woman's honour is her virtue: her virginity or, if married, her loyalty to her husband. A man's is the loyalty of his wife, and, if this is broken, even by no fault of the wife's own (eg. if she is raped), both his and her honour are shattered. Such is the fragility of honour, that even the perception of an indiscretion or a dishonourable act is enough to bring about social death for the party concerned. Importantly, *Fuente Ovejuna* recognises that a sense of honour is due not only to the nobility, but also to commoners. It also shows how the honour system is open to abuse by those of higher rank.

As Esteban, the Mayor of Fuente Ovejuna, recognises, even as the Commander is plotting to have his wicked way with his daughter, Guzmán's rank as a Knight of the Order of Calatrava commands respect. Returning victorious from

Ciudad Real, he is showered with gifts, and when he insists that the councillors sit down in his presence, when honour dictates that they stand, they are most uncomfortable. Guzmán himself, however, is all too aware of the respect due to him, and his sin is to abuse it. The abuse is clear: he insults the town and its people; he aggressively woos Laurencia; and, when unsuccessful, he rapes her, ignoring the sanctity of her marriage, just as he has ignored that of many other women in the town. He also orders that Mengo be whipped black and blue (or, rather, as pink as a salmon steak) for attempting to defend Jacinta's honour as she is dragged away to war. It is not Guzmán's dominance of the town that Lope criticises; it is the abuse of this dominance by the man himself.

Truth to History

The Fuente Ovejuna uprising was an historical fact but, to emphasise the villainy of Guzmán, Lope de Vega inter-mingles it with, and adapts, another true event, that of the invasion of Ciudad Real. Téllez Girón's treachery, in favour of Alfonso V of Portugal, did take place, but Guzmán, whose abuse of Fuente Ovejuna was real according to sixteenth-century chronicles, did not in real life prompt the young Grand Master to attack Ciudad Real. By involving the Commander in this defiance against the Catholic Monarchs, Lope expands Guzmán's dishonourable behaviour, showing him not only as a brutal lord, but also as a disloyal subject, piling more dishonour onto his rank. The proud Commander, whose arrogance is clear from the very beginning of the play, as he indignantly waits for Téllez Girón to attend to him, is so presumptuous as to challenge his own place in the natural order.

It is this natural order to which the play is restored by the end. In the closing scene, it is Ferdinand and Isabella, the Catholic Monarchs still legendary, almost mythical, in Lope's time as the rulers who united Spain, built its empire and secured its place in the world, who mete out justice. Not only do they pardon the people of Fuente Ovejuna, they also forgive the errant Téllez Girón, accepting him back into the fold as part of the restored, secured chain of being. They represent the conduit of the mercy of God, the divine order. Rather than being a 'democratic' play, *Fuente Ovejuna* becomes a play in support of monarchy, but it also sets an example of how those in power should carry out their roles responsibly, respecting the right of their subjects not necessarily to be empowered, but to be governed well. If Lope does challenge the status of the commoner in *Fuente Ovejuna*, it is to challenge the anti-commoner prejudice that was still prevalent in the sixteenth century but was dwindling in the seventeenth; he shows that the humble townspeople, though not of noble rank, are capable of a noble spirit. He depicts a nobility that comprises not only status, but also virtue.

Despite including subtle and challenging debates, often led by female characters, over issues such as sexual harassment, sexual injustice and selfish versus selfless love, Lope's representation of day-to-day rural life is often conventional: *Fuente Ovejuna*'s contemporary audience would have been used to the kind of characters we see in the play, which, in the pastoral tradition, romance each other beside rushing streams, wax lyrical about love, joke about the conventions of the big city, and celebrate weddings with dancing, singing and joviality. Sharp-witted lasses chat with sympathetic, sometimes clown-like lads, and the whole town pays handsome tribute, in its own way, to its rulers. This depiction is a world away from the reality of rural life in Spain at the time of *Fuente Ovejuna*'s writing. The near-complete dominance of feudal lords over the countryside continued well into the seventeenth century, and with peasant farmers increasingly reduced to economic slavery, struggling to live off low yields, a rural exodus was to begin by the 1620s. Aside from Laurencia's witty critique of urban conventions, then, what is seen by some as a comment on the divide between rustic and big-city Spain is at best a lesser subtheme to the overriding, more geographically universal ideas of honour and social order discussed above.

Once the worm turns and the townspeople begin to plan their revenge, some further themes arise, although again, some readings may be more modern than contemporary to the Golden Age. One example is a loosely feminist analysis of *Fuente Ovejuna*: humiliated and violated, Laurencia rails against the men who failed to protect her, and summons the womenfolk of Fuente Ovejuna to take their own part in the town's revenge on Guzmán. Laurencia is certainly the heroine of the piece, with her furiously pained speech after being violated providing a visceral turning-point. Margarita Xirgu, the famous Catalan actress of the early twentieth century, said that the performance of Laurencia could make or break any production of the play. Whether or not Lope intended for Laurencia, Pascuala and her companions' active and equal participation in the frenzied tyrannicide to be a comment on gender equality is open to question. What it does show, however, is another consequence of the breaking of the divine order and the rupture of the sacred bond of marriage. Not only Laurencia, but all of the good, jovial people of Fuente Ovejuna, are transfigured by their suffering at the hands of Guzmán and his men; the triumph of their uprising, or rather its nature, can also be seen as the end result of their dehumanisation. Despite the news that Ferdinand and Isabella are on their way, the townspeople are in no mood to wait, and go after their cruel Commander in the most bloodthirsty fashion, baying for him to be hurled onto a spike to his death, and decapitating him before displaying his head as a trophy. It is only the mythical Catholic Monarchs, almost a deus ex machina, who can, and do, restore order.

Fuente Ovejuna in Performance

Fuente Ovejuna has become one of Lope de Vega's best-known plays, but almost nothing specific is known about its original or early productions. Like Lope's other plays, *Fuente Ovejuna* would no doubt have been staged in the *corrales* of Madrid and other major Spanish cities, the first permanent examples of which were established in the late sixteenth century and which, by the time *Fuente Ovejuna* was written, were thriving.

The *corrales* were outdoor courtyards, enclosed by surrounding houses, and operated at first by the *cofradias*, charitable organisations which, set up to run hospitals, used the income from the *corrales* to fund them. Typically, a stage would be erected at one end of the courtyard, often with a gallery above it, and most of the audience would stand to watch, although some audience members would observe from the windows of surrounding buildings. The public paid on entry (or were supposed to), and the boisterous audience could buy snacks and drinks during the performance, through which they heckled, bickered, and occasionally even brawled.

In many respects, then, the Spanish theatre in Lope's day was not dissimilar to that of his contemporary, Shakespeare, in London, although many well-known Elizabethan theatres, such as the Globe and the Fortune, were purpose-built, with the first such venue, James Burbage's simply-dubbed Theatre, being completed in 1576.

Spanish performances, though popular, were basic in their production values, with only the most primitive of set design elements, and music, when employed, taking place behind a makeshift screen and accompanied by only simple instruments. This seemed to suit Lope, however, who later in his life complained about the technological developments in staging. He lamented how they distracted from the story and saw them as nothing more than an attempt to compensate for bad acting. Costume was a different matter: by the early seventeenth century, Spain's theatre companies had their own costume workshops, making elaborate and impressive costumes, while in Shakespeare's London actors were still wearing the hand-me-downs of their aristocratic patrons. Dancing was a particularly important element of theatre in Spain, with several members of a company often employed purely for their dancing skills. Women were permitted to perform, despite a short-lived, and possibly unenforced, attempt to ban female actors in 1596. Unlike Shakespeare, who wrote female roles for young boys to perform, Lope knew that his heroines would be played by real women.

Fuente Ovejuna's exact date of writing is uncertain: the play was almost certainly written some time after 1609, and was published, along with eleven other plays, in Lope's *Dozena parte*, in 1619. Evidence has been found that *Fuente Ovejuna* may have been performed contemporarily by a troupe of travelling players in Potosí, a major mining town in what is now Bolivia, but aside from this, *Fuente Ovejuna* was just one of many, many plays penned by the prolific Spaniard.

Only in the nineteenth century was interest in *Fuente Ovejuna* revived. The play was translated into French in 1822, and in 1845 the great German Hispanist Adolf Friedrich von Schack published his translation of the text, which he described as 'amongst the most precious jewels' of the Lope canon, in his anthology, *Spanisches Theater*. Not until the end of that century was interest in *Fuente Ovejuna* reignited in Lope's home country of Spain, and only then thanks to academic studies published by Santander-born scholar Marcelino Menéndez y Pelayo.

It was in Russia that the first modern production of *Fuente Ovejuna* took place, in Moscow, on 8 March 1876. Translated into Russian by Sergei Iurev, the play was performed to great acclaim by the Maly Theatre Company, with the legendary Maria Yermalova playing Laurencia. The play caused great controversy: Moscow's chief of police, describing *Fuente Ovejuna* as an invitation to subversion, ordered that the theatre be filled with officers on the second night after revellers left the premiere singing revolutionary anthems. Perhaps unsurprisingly, the popularity of this tale of a people's uprising only increased in Russia as socialism took hold, although even the elitist audience of St Petersburg's Stariinyi Theatre enjoyed a lavish production in 1911, with sets designed by Basque painter Ignacio Zuloaga and folkloric dances advised upon by Catalan musicologist Felip Pedrell. After the Russian Revolution, *Fuente Ovejuna*'s popularity was sealed in Kiev in 1919, when Georgian director Konstantine Marjanishvili staged the play in the Ukrainian capital. To boost Lope's socialist credentials, Marjanishvili opted to cut out the Catholic Monarchs. The change turned *Fuente Ovejuna* into a staple of Soviet theatre for almost twenty years.

Meanwhile, as left- and right-wing sentiments clashed increasingly in Spain, Federico García Lorca's student company, La Barraca, was touring that country's towns and cities, funded by the government and on a mission to bring the Spanish classics back to life for Spaniards of all backgrounds. Premiered in Valencia on 28 June 1933, Lorca's version of *Fuente Ovejuna* became La Barraca's most-often produced play. The company, which tended to modern interpretations of the classics, added popular Andalusian dances called *sevillanas* to the piece, and employed highly symbolic costumes. It also seems that Lorca, like his Soviet counterpart, may have erased Ferdinand and Isabella from the story, contributing to the poet's reputation as a leftist, a reputation which cost him his life only three years later, when he was captured and shot by Franco's fascists.

By the mid-1930s, *Fuente Ovejuna* was re-established at home as a classic. In 1935, the play was performed in the square of Fuente Obejuna (as the town was by then known) itself to mark the tercentenary of Lope's death, and starred Margarita Xirgu, an actress famed across the Spanish-speaking world. The play continued to cause controversy, however, and as the Spanish Civil War brewed, and then broke out, commentators left and right attempted to co-opt *Fuente Ovejuna* to their own cause, with the right accusing those left-wing interpretations of Lope's classic of twisting its meaning and defiling the good name of its author.

The play's popularity spread, and its potential as a political tool rarely went unnoticed. In October 1935, just two weeks after the celebration of a 'day of race' at the Hamburg

Ibero-American Institute, at which Spanish and Nazi German officials stressed the links between their two countries, *Fuente Ovejuna* was staged at the city's Staatliches Schauspielhaus. Praised by one critic as 'the first drama of National Socialism', the play appeared in a heavily adapted version penned by Günter Haenel, entitled *Das brennende Dorf* (*The Blazing Village*) and with the rebellion of the townspeople presented in a less than sympathetic light. *Fuente Ovejuna* was staged in Nazi Germany again in Regensburg in 1939, and was also the only Spanish Golden Age play to be published in Dutch during the Nazi occupation of the Netherlands.

By contrast, the Paris Théâtre du Peuple produced *Fuente Ovejuna* in 1938, in an adaptation by Jean Camp and Jean Cassou. The production was praised by one critic as 'playwriting for the masses', in a review highlighting Laurencia as a sublimely republican character. Georgian ballet master Vakhtang Chabukiani clearly shared this view: in 1939, his ballet, *Laurencia*, premiered in the Soviet Union at St Petersburg's Mariinsky Theatre, based on Lope's original.

Over the 1930s and '40s, *Fuente Ovejuna*'s success continued to grow both at home and abroad, and in 1947 a film version was made, directed by Antonio Román. By the 1950s, translations and productions were proliferating worldwide, with Cuba's Teatro del Pueblo staging *Fuente Ovejuna* in 1960 and 1963, and German playwright Rainer Werner Fassbinder adapting the play in 1970 to show the townspeople descending into a cannibalistic frenzy after taking their revenge. Spanish state television broadcast a TV adaptation in Spain in 1975.

The play has remained a major element of the Spanish theatrical repertoire, with recent productions including a 2005 staging by the Teatre Nacional de Catalunya, in a version by Juan Mayorga. At the time of writing, this production is part of the Spanish Compañía Nacional de Teatro Clásico's current season. Previous to this, the Compañía Nacional de Teatro Clásico staged *Fuente Ovejuna* in 1993, in a version by Carlos Bousoño.

Fuente Ovejuna was first published in English in 1936, in a translation by John Garrett Underhill, and went on to be performed throughout the United Kingdom several times during the twentieth century. Pledging in its manifesto to be 'Manchester's contribution to the forces of democracy', Joan Littlewood's Theatre Union (later reformed as Theatre Workshop) was a likely candidate to stage the classic, and indeed the show was produced by the Mancunian troupe shortly after its founding in 1936. The production of *Fuente Ovejuna* was a direct response to the outbreak of the Spanish Civil War and was intended to draw attention to the plight of the Spanish people. Littlewood's husband and work partner Ewan MacColl recalled how the company 'set Lope's lyrics to the tunes of stirring republican battle songs' and saw *Fuente Ovejuna* as 'a reflection in microcosm of what was actually taking place in Spain'. The characters, said MacColl, 'fought and danced and rioted like a crowd of football enthusiasts expressing their devotion to Manchester United'. Not only was Theatre Union's the first UK production of *Fuente Ovejuna* (perhaps even the first UK production of any play by Lope), it also marked the company's first departure from 'agit-prop-cum-expressionistic' theatre, and won what would become one of the country's most influential theatre collectives a raft of new supporters.

Theatre Union continued to be heavily involved in publicising the plight of those suffering in the Spanish Civil War.

The Glasgow Unity Theatre staged *Fuente Ovejuna* in May 1944, directed by Avrom Greenbaum, at what is now the Citizens' Theatre in the Gorbals, and in 1969 the play was published in a new translation by Alan Sillitoe and Ruth Fainlight, under the title *All Citizens are Soldiers*. Sillitoe and Fainlight's adaptation is set in Spain in 1936, and depicts a group of republican soldiers staging *Fuente Ovejuna* in Madrid. As the play (and the play within the play) continues, the parallels between the Spanish Civil War and the backdrop to the Fuente Ovejuna uprising draw ever closer, merging as *All Citizens are Soldiers* ends: bombs begin to fall, and the actors leave their Golden Age characters behind to fight against the fascists. In 1989, the Royal National Theatre produced *Fuente Ovejuna* in the Cottesloe Theatre; the production, directed by Declan Donnellan and adapted by Adrian Mitchell, represented the United Kingdom at the 1992 Expo in Seville. A radio production was broadcast by the BBC in 2007. The version published here was translated and directed by Laurence Boswell at the Stratford Shakespeare Festival in Ontario, Canada, in 2008.

Translator's Note

This translation was written for a production of *Fuente Ovejuna* at the Shakespeare Festival of Canada, in Stratford, Ontario, which I also directed. Staged in the Tom Patterson Theatre with a cast of thirty-one actors, it was critically well received and enjoyed by enthusiastic audiences.

The main challenge for the Canadian actors in bringing this play to life was much the same as that experienced by actors at the Royal Shakespeare Company in Stratford-upon-Avon, England, where I coordinated and directed a season of Golden Age plays. Actors brought up on Shakespeare have to adjust to Lope's pace. Lope tells a fast and relentless tale, shifting tone, style and plot at breathtaking speed. He does not give his actors as much time or as much information as his English counterpart; he is lean and spare, suggesting a whole character trait or relationship nuance with a single detail. In his writing, everything is subservient to the fast-moving story: character, language and theme are all skillfully engineered to be at the service of his audaciously told tales. This kind of work requires the actors to be sensitive to every detail of the text, and, in performance, to think, feel and move quickly. Once the actors had adjusted to this change of pace they began to relish the material, soon realising that they were being guided by the hand of a playwright who knew how to write challenging parts and thrilling scenes.

I have staged Lope's plays in cities all over Spain and the UK, and for me the greatest pleasure from the Canadian experience was feeling the same emotional residue in the audience at the end of a show. Lope inspires, surprises and enchants an audience, delighting in making them jump with delight and recoil with horror, mixing seriousness with playfulness, making them think, laugh and cry. At the end of a good performance of one of Lope's plays there has always been the same residue, an excited buzz, which is a mixture of emotional exhaustion and delight. In preparing and rehearsing this translation of *Fuente Ovejuna*, it was proved to me once again that Lope tells stories that we still need to hear.

Of course many hands conspire in the process of knocking a script into shape and there are a number of people I want to thank for their part in the creation of this translation. It was originally commissioned by the Stratford Shakespeare Festival, with Antoni Cimolino, Don Shipley and Des McAnuff being brave enough to programme the first ever professional production of a Lope de Vega play in Canada. As I worked on this translation I regularly consulted two inspired Golden Age experts, Katherine Jeffs and Professor Jack Sage; Jack has been helping me to come to grips with Lope de Vega for many years.

As a writer, you don't know how a script really works until it is spoken by actors in a rehearsal room – and then the process of rewriting begins all over again, as the performers test every moment and every syllable. For their rigour and imagination in this part of the process, I want to thank the original cast of the Stratford Festival Company, who helped me to see what worked and what still needed development. Thanks are also due to the stage management team, who worked tirelessly to keep up with the ever-changing nature of the script, and to Robert Blacker, the dramaturg of the Stratford Festival, who gave me many valuable notes during rehearsals. Finally, I have to thank my partner, Sara, and my two children, Lottie and Zinny, who are always a big part of the process from the beginning, as they listen to me beating out the metre on the desk in my study.

Laurence Boswell

Lope de Vega: Key Dates

1562	Lope born in Madrid to Félix de Vega Carpio and Francisca Fernández Flores.
1568	The morisco (converts from Islam to Christianity) rebellion in Alpujarras kills 60,000.
1576	Mutinous Spanish troops sack Antwerp.
c.1577	Lope attends the University of Alcalá de Henares.
1579	The Corral de la Cruz, the first permanent theatre in Madrid, opens.
1580	Dynastic union of the Spanish and Portuguese crowns.
1583	Lope joins naval expedition to take the island of Terceira in the Azores.
1584-5	First recorded instance of women performing on the Spanish stage.
1588	Lope jailed, then exiled from Castile, for writing libellous poetry about producer-director Jerónimo Velázquez and his family; marries Isabel de Urbina; joins the Armada on its failed mission to defeat the English.
1589	Moves to Valencia; already a successful writer, his fame grows.
1590	Moves to Toledo as secretary to the Duke of Alba.
1595	Isabel dies in childbirth.

1596	Failed attempt to ban women from the Spanish stage.
1598	Lope marries Juana de Guardo; Philip II, in mourning for his daughter, bans theatrical productions, but dies that same year and is succeeded by Philip III.
1603	Death of Elizabeth I of England, followed by Anglo-Spanish peace accord.
1604-10	Divides home life between Juana de Guardo and lover, Micaela de Lujón.
1609	Publishes *El arte nuevo de hacer comedias* (*The New Art of Playwriting*).
1613	Juana de Guardo dies.
1614	Joins the priesthood.
1616	Moves to Valencia; begins an affair with Marta de Nevares Santoyo.
1619	Publishes *La dozena parte*, which includes *Fuente Ovejuna*.
1620	Spanish attack in Alsace begins Spain's involvement in the Thirty Years War.
1621	Death of Philip III, succeeded by Philip IV.
1627	Lope awarded a doctorate in theology and receives the St John's Cross from the Pope.
1635	Lope dies.

For Further Reading

Defourneaux, Marcelin, *Daily Life in Spain in the Golden Age* (Chicago: Stanford University Press, 1979)

Domínguez Ortiz, Antonio, & Casey, James (translator), *The Golden Age of Spain, 1516–1659* (London: Weidenfeld and Nicolson, 1971)

Gerstinger, Heinz, & Rosenbaum, Samuel (translator), *Lope De Vega and Spanish Drama* (New York: Frederick Ungar Publishing Co., 1974)

Rennert, Hugo Albert, *The Life of Lope de Vega 1562–1635* (Whitefish: Kessinger Publishing, 2007)

Rennert, Hugo Albert, *The Spanish Stage in the Time of Lope de Vega* (New York: Dover Publications, 1963)

Wilson, Edward M & Muir, Duncan, *A Literary History of Spain. The Golden Age: Drama, 1492–1700* (London/New York: Benn/Barnes & Noble, 1971)

FUENTE OVEJUNA

Characters

ESTEBAN, *Mayor of Fuente Ovejuna*
ALONSO, *an Alderman of Fuente Ovejuna*
JUAN ROJO, *a councillor of Fuente Ovejuna*
FRONDOSO, *a young peasant boy, son of Juan Rojo*
MENGO, *a shepherd*
BARRILDO, *a peasant boy, friend of Frondoso*
LEONELO, *a student from Salamanca University*
FIRST ALDERMAN *of Ciudad Real*
SECOND ALDERMAN *of Ciudad Real*
KING FERDINAND OF ARAGON
JUDGE, *an official of the court of Ferdinand*
DON MANRIQUE, *Grand Master of the Order of Santiago*
DON RODRIGO TÉLLEZ GIRÓN, *Grand Master of the Order of Calatrava* (MASTER)
DON FERNÁN GÓMEZ DE GUZMÁN, *Chief Commander of the Order of Calatrava* (COMMANDER)
FLORES, *his Captain*
ORTUÑO, *his Sergeant*
CIMBRANOS, *one of his troops*

LAURENCIA, *a young peasant girl, daughter of Esteban*
PASCUALA, *a young peasant girl, friend of Laurencia*
JACINTA, *a young peasant girl, friend of Laurencia and Pascuala*
QUEEN ISABELLA OF CASTILE

SOLDIERS
MUSICIANS
CITIZENS *of Fuente Ovejuna*
COURTIERS

ACT ONE

Scene One

Almagro. Spring, 1476. The residence of the GRAND MASTER, *the Order of Calatrava.*

COMMANDER.
Are you sure the Master knows I'm
In Almagro?

FLORES.
                        Sir, he knows!

ORTUÑO.
Old enough now to keep you waiting.

COMMANDER.
Does he know the man who's waiting
Is Fernán Gómez de Guzmán?

FLORES.
He's nineteen, sir, don't be surprised.

COMMANDER.
He may have forgotten my name
But I'm still his Chief Commander
And that title demands respect.

ORTUÑO.
He's surrounded by advisors
Saying, 'Go on, keep him waiting.'

COMMANDER.
    He'll win few friends playing that game.
    When you treat a man with respect
    You build a bridge into his heart
    When you treat a man with contempt
    You make an enemy for life.

ORTUÑO.
    If the discourteous man knew
    How all his colleagues despise him
    And dream of a thousand ways of
    Making him grovel in the dirt
    Wouldn't he rather end his days
    Than go on living such a life?

FLORES.
    A man like that's a total bore!
    A vile, tedious waste of time!
    When you treat an equal badly
    You show the world you're a fool
    You treat those beneath you badly
    You show the heart of a tyrant.
    But in this case there's no offence
    Just a boy who has yet to learn
    The importance of courtesy.

COMMANDER.
    The day they pinned the sacred cross
    Of our crusade on his young breast
    He swore an oath compelling him
    To treat all men with courtesy.

FLORES.
    Well, if he's been briefed against you
    Now's your chance to change his thinking.

ORTUÑO.

Look sharp, I can see him coming.

COMMANDER.

Time to find out what he's made of.

Enter the GRAND MASTER, *accompanied.*

MASTER.

Don Fernán Gómez de Guzmán
I humbly beg your forgiveness
I have only just been informed
Of your presence in Almagro.

COMMANDER.

I have good reason to feel wronged.
I had hoped my loyalty and my
Years of service would teach you
To treat me with respect: as you're
The Grand Master of Calatrava
And I, your High Commander,
Am your servant and your slave.

MASTER.

I was not informed of your arrival,
Accept my apology, once more:
Accept my embrace.

COMMANDER.

                      You honour me
As you should, how often have I
Risked my life on your behalf
In these dangerous times?
And who intervened with His Holiness
When the question of your youth
Put your succession in doubt?

MASTER.

You did and I swear, by the cross
Which graces both our breasts, I am
Grateful for your loyal service
I honour you as a father.

COMMANDER.

My humble thanks, I am content.

MASTER.

Now, what news of the war?

COMMANDER.

                    Let me
Show you where the path of duty lies.

MASTER.

Speak, I am ready to listen.

COMMANDER.

Don Rodrigo Téllez Girón,
Grand Master of Calatrava:
I remember the day your father
Gave up that title and proposed
That you should succeed him.
I remember an eight-year-old boy
Swearing a vow of allegiance,
His election confirmed on oath
By a host of High Commanders,
Six anointed Kings, and Pius
The Holy Father of Rome.
I remember a boy of sixteen
Weeping as he buried his uncle,
His loyal regent, Juan Pacheco,
Grand Master of Santiago.

I watched that boy take up
The heavy burden of power
And today I address the youth
Who must make a man's decision.
Since the death of King Enrique
One question has echoed through our land:
'Who should sit on the throne of Castile?'
Ferdinand, Great King of Aragon,
Makes his claim through his marriage
To Isabel, Enrique's sister.
But your family support Alfonso,
King of Portugal, and his claim
Through his wife Princess Juanna,
Enrique's only natural child;
Blood and honour demand that you
Support your cousin Alfonso's cause,
And to that end I have come here
To urge you, Master, to assemble
All the Knights of Calatrava
And take Ciudad Real: a place of
Vital strategic significance
Forming as it does a gateway
Between Andalusia and Castile!
Minimal force will be required,
The city is defended by a handful
Of civilians and a collection
Of minor nobility: Master,
It's time to silence those who claim
That the crimson cross you wear
Is too heavy for your young shoulders.
Remember the counts of Uruena,
From whom you draw most noble blood,

And let their triumphs drive you on
To heights of even greater glory!
Remember the Lords of Villena
And all the brave generals of that line,
Whose many victories are almost
Too numerous to be carried aloft,
Even on the wings of Fame herself!
It's time for you to go to war
And dip your, as yet, untried sword
In the blood of your enemies!
Let its blade match the cross on your breast
For how can I truly call you
Master of the Holy Cross when
One is crimson and the other white?
It's time, Rodrigo, for you to write
Your own burning page in the proud history
Of your illustrious kinsmen!

MASTER.

Commander, you may be sure
I know where my duty lies:
I will support my cousin's claim,
For I can see his cause is just.
I will lay siege to Ciudad Real,
And you will see me breach its walls
Like a bolt of fire from Heaven!
I'll silence those who dare to say
That I buried my courage
The day I buried my uncle.
I will unsheathe my sword and its
White blade will shine as red as this
Proud cross on my breast when it drips
With the blood of our enemies!

How many troops can you supply
To support me in this conflict?

COMMANDER.
Very few. I've an elite group of men
Who will fight for you like lions.
I live in Fuente Ovejuna,
A little town in the mountains,
The peasant inhabitants of which
Are happy digging muddy fields,
But are hardly qualified
To march with you to battle.

MASTER.
And you live in that place?

COMMANDER.
                    In these
Turbulent times, it's a safe place
In which to build a stronghold.

MASTER.
Let your men prepare for battle.

COMMANDER.
Not one of them will shirk your call.

MASTER.
I'll mount my horse and lift my lance:
We march on Ciudad Real, today!

Exit all.

Scene Two

Beside the well, on the outskirts of Fuente Ovejuna.

Enter LAURENCIA *and* PASCUALA.

LAURENCIA.
    Well, I hope he never comes back!

PASCUALA.
    Well, I'm surprised, I imagined
    When I told you he'd gone off to fight,
    You'd be disappointed, distressed.

LAURENCIA.
    I wish Fuente Ovejuna
    Had never seen that man's face.

PASCUALA.
    Laurencia, I've known girls as
    Fierce as you, indeed some fiercer,
    Who tried to resist his advances,
    But whose hearts melted like butter.

LAURENCIA.
    Pascuala, do you know other girls
    Whose hearts are as hard as oak?

PASCUALA.
    Oh, please, which of us can say, 'Not me,'
    You never know what might happen!

LAURENCIA.
    It will never happen to me!
    No matter what anyone thinks.

If I gave our Commander what
He's after: Would he marry me?

PASCUALA.

No!

LAURENCIA.
So, there is nothing to discuss!
This town is full of women who
Believed his promises and woke
To find their reputations ruined
And their pillows wet with tears.

PASCUALA.
My friend, you'll need a miracle
To escape that monster's claws.

LAURENCIA.
It's not so hard: he's been chasing
Me for a month now and when
I see him coming I turn away
Or cast my eyes into the dirt.
His pimp, Captain Flores, and the
Sly old fox, Sergeant Ortuño,
Tried to tempt me with expensive gifts,
A necklace, a pair of shoes, a dress;
They pushed me against a tree and
Whispered such tales of their master,
That I confess, I was afraid.
But all this attention won't change
My resolution, I don't want him!

PASCUALA.
Where did they catch up with you?

LAURENCIA.
By the river. Six days ago.

PASCUALA.
They'll persuade you in the end.

LAURENCIA.

Me?

PASCUALA.
Well, I didn't mean the parish priest!

LAURENCIA.
This is one war Guzmán won't win.
I prefer to talk of more important
Things, like breakfast, a sweet slice
Of bacon roasted on the fire
Slipped inside a fistful of bread
Torn from a loaf I baked myself
Washed down with a cup of cold wine
Stolen from my mother's old jar.
At lunchtime, I like to watch
Hunks of rabbit changing dancing
Partners in the bubbling gravy,
And when I stumble home at night
Exhausted and a little peckish
I like to arrange the marriage
Of a finely chopped aubergine
And an eligible slice of ham:
Then as I'm preparing supper
I like to pluck a handful of grapes –
Please God protect the vine from hail –
And graze on them before we dine,
On a mountain of suckling pig

With red peppers soaked in olive oil:
And when I finally climb the stairs
I like to get down on my knees
And speak to my maker, 'Dear Lord,
Lead me not into temptation.'
You see, I prefer all this, my life,
To the lies and flattery spoken
With such persistence by those thugs.
And what's all this pursuit about,
What do men actually want from us?
To lay us naked on a sheet
And when they're done to run away
With exactly the same haste
With which they tried to seduce us.

PASCUALA.
Laurencia, it's true! When men
Fall out of love with us they behave
Like the ungrateful house sparrows
Towards the farmer's wife in the spring:
In winter when the fields are white,
The cold little creatures fly down
From the rooftops, hungry for food,
So ravenous they'll eat the crumbs
Directly from her big old hands
But when the winter packs its bags
And the fields don their suits of green
The birds forget their winter friend.
She no longer hears them singing
'Give me, give me, give me food.' No!
When they can find things to eat elsewhere,
From the roof she hears them taunting:
'Silly, silly, silly, old fool.'

And men are the same: when they want us
They stare into our eyes and say:
'You're the one, my love, my life: You,
My divine, radiant goddess!'
But when the fires of passion cool
We no longer hear them singing,
'Baby, baby, cheep, cheep, please.' No!
Then it's: 'Easy, easy! Cheap! Please.'

LAURENCIA.

Men! Don't believe a thing they say.

PASCUALA.

No. I don't. Not a single word!

Enter BARRILDO, MENGO *and* FRONDOSO.

FRONDOSO.

Barrildo, it's a discussion.
Please, keep a sense of proportion.

BARRILDO.

Look, I see someone who'll help us,
Let's ask them to make a judgement.

MENGO.

Before you go and speak to them
Can we negotiate a deal?
So when they decide in my favour
You both give me some money,
My reward for being right.

BARRILDO.

Sure, Mengo, we'd be delighted:
But if you lose, what do we get?

MENGO.
> Equal shares in my box fiddle:
> It's worth more than a barn full of grain,
> Yeah, well, it's worth that much to me!

BARRILDO.
> Fine. Deal.

FRONDOSO.
> I'll talk to the judges.
> Cordial greetings, fair ladies.

LAURENCIA.
> Ladies, Frondoso, why call us ladies?

FRONDOSO.
> I'm following the city fashion.
> In the city everything's upside down:
> Important people are never rude,
> They're just overworked or busy,
> Their arrogance is confidence,
> Their cynicism is gritty,
> Their bald heads are distinguished and
> Their big feet are firm foundations.
> They tell lies and it's pragmatic,
> And when they're vain, it's rather charming.
> A duke who's drinking himself to death
> Is awfully good company,
> A lord who abuses women
> Is something of a ladies' man,
> A marquis who gets the pox
> Is said to have a minor rash,
> And a count who catches the plague
> Has acquired a summer cold.
> So, when I called you ladies

I was talking in this fashion,
Of which, I think we've had enough.
Though I could go on for ever.

LAURENCIA.
That's how they talk in the city
When it suits them to be polite,
But they use another language
When they don't have to hide what they mean.

FRONDOSO.
Are we going to hear a sample?

LAURENCIA.
It's not flattery: In the city
A serious man is a bore,
An outspoken man is a fool,
A kindly man is a weakling,
A generous man wants something,
A humble man is a pushover,
And a good, honest soul is a peasant.
Be loyal and you are stubborn,
Be concerned and you're nosy,
Be patient and you're a coward,
Be polite, you're up to something.
If you're talented, you just got lucky,
If you're unlucky, you had it coming.
A women who says 'No' is frigid,
With an opinion, she's a shrew,
She wants to look good, she's a tart,
She wants to live an honest life:
You know, I think I've said enough.

MENGO.
The devil's in you, young lady!

BARRILDO.
    That was an amazing outburst.

MENGO.
    She's a tongue like a butcher's knife.

LAURENCIA.
    Weren't you arguing about something?
    Didn't you want us to sort it out?

FRONDOSO.
    Yes, that's right, we do.

LAURENCIA.
                        So, speak!

FRONDOSO.
    Laurencia, listen closely.

LAURENCIA.
    I'm listening, with both ears.

FRONDOSO.
    We're counting on your common sense.

LAURENCIA.
    Good, who was arguing with whom?

FRONDOSO.
    Barrildo and me against Mengo.

LAURENCIA.
    And what is Mengo's problem?

BARRILDO.
    He denies something that cannot
    Be denied, but still he denies it.

MENGO.
 I deny it, because I know I'm right.

LAURENCIA.
 What does he deny?

BARRILDO.
                    That love exists.

LAURENCIA.
 Well, that's an extreme position.

BARRILDO.
 Yes, extremely stupid. Listen:
 Love is the basis of everything,
 The world wouldn't work without it.

MENGO.
 I'm not a skilled philosopher,
 In fact, I can't actually read,
 But if the stuff we are made of –
 Blood, phlegm, choler, melancholy –
 Are elements always at war,
 Doesn't that tell you something?

BARRILDO.
 The world above us and the world
 Here below are bound together
 In the purest love, in concord,
 Which is the harmony of love.

MENGO.
 At this point I'd like to make clear
 I don't deny the existence
 Of divine love, Barrildo.
 However, there is something else,

A force inside each one of us,
Which reveals what we truly are:
My hand will deflect any blow
Aimed at my sweet, handsome face.
My feet will run me out of harm's way.
My eyelid will snap shut at the
First hint of danger to my eye.
This is a selfish, human love,
Which is something I don't deny.

PASCUALA.
So, what are you trying to prove?

MENGO.
That love between people is selfish.
That people look out for themselves.

PASCUALA.
I don't agree, what of the love
Which binds a man and woman?
Are you telling us that all that
Is nothing but selfishness?

MENGO.
It is selfish love, not selfless.
What is this love you describe?

LAURENCIA.
A desire for beauty.

MENGO.
                    I see.
And why does love desire beauty?

LAURENCIA.
To enjoy it.

MENGO.
                To enjoy it.
    So, love seeks beauty because it
    Takes pleasure from that beauty?

LAURENCIA.
                                    Yes.

MENGO.
    So love pursues its own self-interest
    Seeking out what will give it pleasure?

LAURENCIA.
    Yes, it does.

MENGO.
                So, there we have it!
    The love of human beings is selfish,
    Self-absorbed and self-regarding:
    We hunt beauty for our own ends.

BARRILDO.
    Last Sunday in his sermon
    Father Pedro quoted Plato:
    'The lover should devote himself
    To the virtue and soul of the
    Beloved': that made sense to me.

PASCUALA.
    I think we're out of our depth here!
    This conversation would have all
    The smartest professors in Spain
    Scratching their heads for an answer.

LAURENCIA.
    Pascuala's right, so stop wasting time

Wrestling with Mengo's nonsense.
And Mengo, you'd better thank God
That He didn't make you for love.

MENGO.
Are you in love?

LAURENCIA.

With my honour.

FRONDOSO.
May your heart ache with jealousy.

BARRILDO.
So, who wins?

PASCUALA.

Best talk to the priest,
Or the sexton, he'll sort this out:
Laurencia just told you she's not
In love, and I know nothing of it,
So how can we make a judgement?

FRONDOSO.
Her contempt is my judgement.

Enter FLORES.

FLORES.
May God protect you, good people.

LAURENCIA.
Where have you flown in from, Captain?

FLORES.
Doesn't my armour give a clue?

LAURENCIA.
Is the Commander coming home?

FLORES.

> The battle cost a lot of blood
> And the lives of some dear comrades:
> But we're home now, the fighting's done.

FRONDOSO.

> Captain, tell us what happened?

FLORES.

> These eyes were witness to it all,
> So, who can report it better?
> To storm the city of Ciudad Real
> Our bold young Master summoned
> Seven thousand proud men-at-arms
> From among his loyal subjects,
> And six hundred knights on horseback
> From among his holy brothers:
> For the Order of Calatrava
> Demands military service
> Of all who wear its crimson cross
> And share its holy mission:
> To drive the Moors out of our land!
> Our handsome leader rode out
> In a surcoat of emerald green,
> Decorated with embroidered monograms
> And at the elbow bracelets hung,
> Linked with frogs wrought in gold.
> He sat astride a mighty stallion,
> High-spirited and dapple-grey,
> Who'd grown up drinking the clear water
> Of the Guadalquivir, and eating
> The lush green grass that grows upon
> Its fertile banks: White silk ribbons

Plaited his frosty mane and strips
Of doeskin knit his pallid tail,
Which seemed to match the snowdrifts
Of his fetlocks and flanks: Beside him
Rode your lord, Fernán Gómez,
On a giant, honey-coloured steed
With jet-black hooves and tail
And a lower lip of white.
Over a suit of Turkish chain mail
Were buckled gleaming breastplates and
An orange surcoat trimmed with pearls:
Above all this his helmet was crowned
With a spray of white plumes, which seemed
The blossom to the orange of his coat.
In his strong arms, which were tied with
White rosettes, he carried a mighty lance,
As large as the trunk of the giant ash,
From which it had been hewn, the sight
Of which makes Granada shake with fear.
The city armed itself, swore its loyalty
To Ferdinand and Isabella,
Declared that they would give their lives
To remain their subjects: they offered
Brave and sustained resistance:
But to no avail. The Master rode
Into the city, victorious,
And ordered the beheading of
All noblemen who'd slandered his name,
While prisoners of lesser rank
Were gagged and then whipped through the streets,
An example to their fellow citizens.
Rodrigo is Master now in Ciudad Real,

Loved and feared in equal measure,
And those who talk of such things predict
A golden future for a young man who can
Conquer and punish with such force:
They say many a blue crescent moon
Will fall before the power of his
Crimson cross: He gave so generously
To all who'd fought beside him, not least
His Commander and his Captain,
It seemed he was giving from his own purse,
Not sacking some fallen city.
That song celebrates your lord's return.
Go and cheer him home, for the love
Of the common people, is the
Fairest laurel to grace the victor's brow!

Exit all.

Scene Three

The town square in Fuente Ovejuna.

Enter COMMANDER, SOLDIERS, ESTEBAN,
ALONSO, MUSICIANS *and* CITIZENS *of Fuente Ovejuna.*

MUSICIANS (*singing*).
    So welcome home
    Our great Commander,
    From the conquering of lands
    And the killing of men.
    Vivan los Guzmánes!
    Vivan los Girónes!

He's gentle in peacetime
When soft are his words.
But when he is fighting
Beware of his sword.
From Ciudad Real
He comes home a hero,
With blood-spattered armour
And bags full of plunder.
Viva muchos años,
Viva Fernán Gómez!

COMMANDER.

My good people, I am duty bound to thank you
For the love you have shown me with this welcome.

ALONSO.

We show only a part of what we truly feel.
Commander, can you be surprised at such a welcome?
It is what you deserve.

ESTEBAN.

                    On behalf of our community
And its councillors whom you honour with your presence
We ask, indeed, we beg you, to accept the tributes
Which burden the carts and crates that stand before you:
We make this offering with some shame because, though
These gifts are given from the heart, they are home-made.
First, two baskets full of earthenware crockery.
A flock of geese, who it seems would like to prolong
The choral tribute, which was sung for your welcome.
Over here a brace of salted pigs, mighty beasts,
And a fine selection of offal and cured ham,
The scent of which is as sweet to us as any glove

Perfumed in amber: in these crates a hundred pairs
Of capons and hens, the recruitment of which has
Left the roosters of many villages and hamlets
Hereabout helpless, heartbroken, and alone.
They have no weapons to give you, no warhorses
Draped in cloth of embroidered gold: they have only
The love that lives in their hearts, which is gold, pure gold.
Talking of purity, my lord, I give you my word
That in these dozen wineskins is liquor so strong
That should your soldiers drink it they will find themselves
Happy to do guard duty completely naked
On the coldest January night, they will need
No swords, this firewater will so steel their souls.
Of the cheeses, goat and sheep, and all the other
Local specialties: scented honey, flan,
Rabbit pie, blood sausage and cake, I'll say no more.
These gifts are tokens of the love of your people:
May you and your household enjoy them, every one.

COMMANDER.

Mayor, town councillors, my people:
I'm very grateful. And farewell.

ALONSO.

My lord, you must be exhausted.
Do go inside and take your rest.
As you go, please note, we've covered
The path to your door with fresh reeds
And bulrushes; if the budget
Had stretched to it you can be sure
We would have emblazoned your gates
With emeralds and pearls – you deserve
As much and more, so very much more.

COMMANDER.
>I'm sure that's true. I'm very pleased.
>Farewell.

ESTEBAN.
>Singers, take a deep breath.
>Let's hear that stirring song once more.

MUSICIANS (*singing*).
>So welcome home
>Our great Commander
>From the conquering of lands
>And the killing of men.
>*Vivan los Guzmánes,*
>*Vivan los Girónes,*
>*Viva muchos años,*
>*Viva Fernán Gómez!*

Exit all but COMMANDER, LAURENCIA, PASCUALA, FLORES *and* ORTUÑO.

COMMANDER.
>Hold it. You two. I want a word.

LAURENCIA.
>What is your lordship's command?

COMMANDER.
>Last week, I passed you in the street:
>I smiled, you looked the other way.

LAURENCIA.
>Pascuala, that was rude of you.

PASCUALA.
>Me? Rude to the Commander? No.

COMMANDER.

I was talking to you, proud one.
Do you not belong to me?
And your friend there, the milkmaid.
Are you not my property?

PASCUALA.

We are, but
Perhaps not in the way you'd like.

COMMANDER.

Come inside, there's nothing to fear.
There are many men in my house.

LAURENCIA.

If the Mayor had been invited,
As he is my father, I'd be
Happy to come inside.

COMMANDER.

Flores!

FLORES.

Sir!

COMMANDER.

How dare they disobey me?

FLORES.

Get inside!

LAURENCIA.

Get your hands off me!

FLORES.

Come in. Think about it!

PASCUALA.
                    I did!
  We go inside. You lock the door.

FLORES.
  Calm down. He just wants to show you
  Some of the presents he's brought home.

COMMANDER (*aside*).
  Ortuño, if you get them inside,
  Lock the door.

ORTUÑO (*aside*).
                    Of course I will.

LAURENCIA.
  Captain Flores, out of my way.

ORTUÑO.
  Think of yourself as a tribute,
  Like a peach, or a lump of cheese.

PASCUALA.
  Let me get past you or I'll bite.

FLORES.
  Forget it! They're a pair of snakes.

LAURENCIA.
  Hasn't he had enough today?
  His house is full of meat.

ORTUÑO.
                    But it's
  Your sweet morsel he'd like to chew!

LAURENCIA.
  I hope he eats until he bursts.

Exit LAURENCIA *and* PASCUALA.

FLORES.

We didn't quite fulfil our brief.
I don't want to go back in there:
When we turn up empty-handed
You know how he'll chew our heads off.

ORTUÑO.

That's how life is for a servant.
If you want to survive it, Captain,
Keep your head down and keep smiling.
Can't handle it? Do something else!

Exit all.

Scene Four

The Royal Court in Toledo.

KING FERDINAND *and* QUEEN ISABELLA *with* DON
MANRIQUE, *Master of Santiago, and* COURTIERS.

ISABELLA.

We must take decisive action.
King Alfonso has gathered
A significant body of troops
On our Portuguese border.
If we strike now we will gain the
Initiative, if we delay we
Leave ourselves open to attack.

FERDINAND.

We can rely on solid support
From Navarre and Aragon and

When we've resolved the conflict here,
In Castile, we can move forward
With all confidence and speed.

ISABELLA.

Indeed, my lord, all our plans depend
On securing peace in Castile.

MANRIQUE.

Two aldermen from Ciudad Real
Would like to speak with you.
My lord, what shall I say to them?

FERDINAND.

We will not deny them our presence.

Enter two ALDERMEN *of Ciudad Real.*

ALDERMAN 1.

Ferdinand, great Catholic King,
Sent by the grace of Heaven
From Aragon to be our guide
And our salvation in Castile:
We come in all humility
In the name of Ciudad Real
To beg your royal protection.
We were proud and happy to live
Under your jurisdiction but
A cruel fate has stripped us
Of that precious privilege.
Don Rodrigo Téllez Girón,
The Master of Calatrava,
Who has earned himself a name
As a strong and powerful leader,
Keen perhaps to add more honour

To the reputation of his order,
Has laid siege to our city.
Our troops offered brave resistance
Fighting with such determination
That the gutters of our streets
Flowed with the blood of the fallen.
Rodrigo prevailed: his victory
Could not have been achieved without
The leadership and advice of
Don Fernán Gómez de Guzmán.
Rodrigo now governs our city
And we must be his subjects,
Unless you can take measures
To reverse this situation.

FERDINAND.
Where is Fernán Gómez now?

ALDERMAN 1.
We believe, in Fuente Ovejuna,
A small town in the foothills
Of the mountains of Morena.
He has a home and stronghold there.
He treats the people of that town
In ways that decency forbids us
To describe, depriving them
Of all happiness and justice.

FERDINAND.
Where are your leaders?

ALDERMAN 2.
                    My lord,
We have no leaders: few of our

Men survived this attack; they were
Imprisoned, or wounded, or killed.

ISABELLA.

We must act without delay,
We cannot allow the momentum
Of victory to inspire
The young Master to deeds of
Even greater audacity. My lord,
The loss of Ciudad Real gives
King Alfonso a gateway into
The very heart of our territory.

FERDINAND.

Don Manrique, you will take
Two battalions of infantry
And put down this rebellion
With all speed and without mercy.
The Count of Cabra, Don Diego
De Córdoba, will ride with you,
A soldier known to all the world
For his fortitude and courage.
This would seem to be the most
Effective use of our resources.

MANRIQUE.

Your Majesty, this bold response
Shows customary strength and vision.
I'll curb this young man's arrogance
Or I will die in the attempt.

ISABELLA.

With our enterprise in your hands
We are confident of success.

Exit all.

Scene Five

A wooded glade on the side of a mountain, outside Fuente Ovejuna.

Enter LAURENCIA *and* FRONDOSO.

LAURENCIA.
   I left my washing by the stream,
   Only half wrung out, because I need
   To speak to you, here, in private;
   Frondoso, you have gone too far!
   The way you were looking at me
   Down there was enough to get every
   Tongue in the village whispering:
   He fancies her, she fancies him.
   Everything will be debated!
   And as you're not a bad-looking boy
   With some kind of style and spirit,
   Who dresses perhaps a little
   Better than some of the others,
   There isn't a maid churning butter
   Or a boy out tending his goats
   Who hasn't assumed the right
   To discuss the date of our wedding!
   They behave as if the priest had
   Already called the banns, given us
   His bassoon solo, blessed the rings
   And asked us both to say 'I do'.
   Well, good luck to them I say,
   I hope that when harvest comes around
   Their barns will be full of wheat and
   Their vats will be full of new wine, and
   They don't regret wasting their time
   In idle speculation and gossip!

But it means nothing to me, nothing.
I'm not bothered. I don't give a damn!

FRONDOSO.

Loving a woman as cruel and
As beautiful as you isn't easy.
I shake when I see you coming,
I tremble when I hear your voice.
I have one hope, to marry you:
Is this a reasonable response
To my honest love and devotion?

LAURENCIA.

It's the only response I've got!

FRONDOSO.

Every minute I think of you,
I close my eyes and I see you,
I try to sleep and I dream of you.
I can't eat, or drink, or find rest.
And when those angelic eyes
Look on me with indifference:
Help, Heaven! I'm losing my mind!

LAURENCIA.

Then get yourself to a doctor!

FRONDOSO.

You are my doctor, my sickness
And my cure: imagine us as
A pair of doves, perched on a branch,
Beak in feather, feather in beak,
Singing together in bliss after
The priest has made us man and wife.

LAURENCIA.

Frondoso, speak to my uncle:
I'm not in love but I might be
Acquiring some of the symptoms.

FRONDOSO.

Look over there! The Commander!

LAURENCIA.

Out hunting deer in the forest.
Go and hide behind those bushes.

FRONDOSO.

How will I hide my jealous heart?

Enter the COMMANDER, *with crossbow.*

COMMANDER.

My lucky day! On the trail of
A timid buck, I come across
A most attractive young doe.

LAURENCIA.

Sir, I was doing my washing
By the stream, I came here to rest.
And now, with your permission, sir,
I'll go back and finish my work.

COMMANDER.

My beautiful Laurencia,
This crude response is an insult
To the grace with which Heaven has
Blessed you, it distorts your features,
Makes you seem like a monster.
Until today you've avoided
My loving entreaties, but here,

These silent, sheltering trees
Will tell no tales: why should you be
The only girl in the village
Too proud to return my smile?
You know, young Sebastiana,
The wife of Pedro Redondo,
She returned my smile and more, much
More, and your good friend Innes,
She found her way to my bed two days
After she'd sworn her vows in church.

LAURENCIA.

Sir, with respect, if those women
Found the way to give you pleasure,
It is perhaps because they'd walked
That path so many times before
And with so many other men.
May Heaven bless your sport and please
Leave me alone. Stop hunting me!
If it weren't for the cross on your chest,
Sir, I'd take you for the devil!

COMMANDER.

What an infuriating response.
I'll put my crossbow on the ground,
And let's see if these hands can't melt
That proud, frigid heart.

LAURENCIA.

               What's this!
My lord! Remember who you are!

COMMANDER.

Come! Don't resist me!

FRONDOSO (*aside*).

                    If I raise
This crossbow from the ground, I swear
I will use it if I have to.

COMMANDER.
  Stop. Don't fight.

LAURENCIA.

                   Heaven, help me!

COMMANDER.
  We're alone here, don't be afraid.

FRONDOSO.
  Noble lord! If you don't release
  That innocent girl, I swear my
  Rage will overcome my respect
  For that holy cross on your breast
  And this bolt will splinter your heart.

COMMANDER.
  Peasant, dog!

FRONDOSO.

            Peasant, yes! Dog, no!
  Laurencia. Run.

LAURENCIA.

             Frondoso!
  Be careful. You must. Take care.

FRONDOSO.

                    Go!

Exit LAURENCIA.

COMMANDER (*aside*).
 The man is a fool who leaves home
 Without buckling on his sword!
 Ironic: I didn't wear it
 Lest I'd frighten off my prey.

FRONDOSO.
 My lord, if I release this bolt:
 You'll fall like a stricken deer.

COMMANDER.
 Peasant lout, the girl has gone now,
 Put down my crossbow. Put it down!
 Do you hear me, boy?

FRONDOSO.
                    No, my lord!
 A man in love is deaf to all insults.
 And I'd be a fool to put this down:
 You'd just pick it up and kill me.

COMMANDER.
 Do you think a man of my rank
 Could turn his back and walk away,
 Retreat before a peasant child?
 Stand fast and shoot me though the heart.
 I won't break my oath of chivalry!

FRONDOSO.
 I don't ask that, I understand
 The obligation of your rank.
 But I've my own obligations:
 One of which is to stay alive,
 So, I'll take your crossbow and leave.

Exit FRONDOSO.

COMMANDER.
   I'll have revenge on that peasant
   For his insult and his intrusion!
   But why didn't I wrestle him
   To the ground and break his neck?
   What's this? What's this? I'm burning with shame.

Exit COMMANDER.

. *End of Act One.*

ACT TWO

Scene One

The town square in Fuente Ovejuna.

Enter ESTEBAN *and* ALONSO.

ESTEBAN.
  It's obvious! The weather's not been good this year
  And doesn't look like improving any time soon,
  So we stop depleting our reserve stocks of grain
  Or we'll have nothing left when winter comes around:
  Why isn't this clear to all our council members?

ALONSO.
  In my time on the committee, prudent planning
  Has always proved to be the best way to govern.

ESTEBAN.
  Well, we'll have to take this up with the Commander.
  Can I tell you what makes me really angry?
  Astrologers: who, though they know less than nothing,
  Claim, in long and incoherent dissertations,
  To have access to secrets known only to God!
  They speak with the authority of archbishops
  About what has and what shall soon come to pass, but
  When you want an answer to a simple question
  You find that the best of them is worse than useless!
  Are their libraries full of moons and spinning planets?

It would appear their skulls are full of fluffy clouds.
How can they really know what's going on up there?
And how dare they alarm us with their speculations
And their oh-so-precise instructions, regarding
Which crop to sow, how and when, wheat here, barley
     there,
No to mustard, yes to cucumbers and pumpkins?
There are pumpkins in my garden with bigger brains!
They foretell the death of an important person
And lo, a king drops dead in Transylvania.
They say there will be lots of beer in Germany,
It will almost definitely rain in England,
You can be sure of bright sunshine in Morocco,
But do beware of biting frost in Russia!
Let me give you a prediction: if we plant now
Or never, the year will still end in December.

Enter LEONELO *and* BARRILDO.

LEONELO.
It looks like someone beat us to our favourite spot.
So, where are we going to sit and have a chat?

BARRILDO.
How was university?

LEONELO.
                    That's a long story.

BARRILDO.
You'll soon be a lawyer and make lots of money!

LEONELO.
Let's see. I'll end up making less than the barber.
What we were just discussing is common knowledge.

BARRILDO.
  You've come home with a brain bulging with ideas.

LEONELO.
  I studied the subjects that seemed most important.

BARRILDO.
  So many books are published these days that every
  Village square is full of self-proclaimed professors.

LEONELO.
  Yes, but has printing expanded or shrunk the sea
  Of human knowledge? You know, I think the latter.
  Ideas were once condensed in handy summaries
  Today so much hot air is published, people get lost.
  Try to keep abreast of everything that's printed
  You get brain ache from information overload.
  Only fools would deny that amongst all the dross,
  Printing has made known the work of some great minds,
  Preserved their thoughts against the ravages of time,
  Spread their benevolent influence round the world:
  But some poor souls, whose work was thought important,
  Have had their reputations destroyed by publication:
  And some dishonest hacks have borrowed the name
  Of our best playwright to get their work into print:
  Whilst a few malicious souls have deliberately
  Written rubbish and sent it out into the world
  In the name of an enemy they seek to destroy!
  Printing is not only a force for good, my friend.

BARRILDO.
  My friend, I disagree . . .

LEONELO.
                              Is it right that spiteful fools

Can damage the reputations of learned men?

BARRILDO.
   But surely printing represents some kind of progress?

LEONELO.
   Hundreds of years have passed happily without it!
   Has this age of books thrown up an Aristotle?
   Has a profusion of print produced a new Plato?

BARRILDO.
   I've clearly trodden on a corn with this, my friend.
   Perhaps we should talk about something else. A seat!

Enter JUAN ROJO *and* PEASANT.

JUAN.
   Yes, people who know nothing about the subject
   May gossip and cry 'Miser', but I can tell you:
   These days, you need to sell your farm and livestock
   Before you can give a girl a proper dowry!

PEASANT.
   What news of the Commander? I'm sorry! What's wrong?

JUAN.
   Didn't you hear how he treated Laurencia?

PEASANT.
   The world never knew a more lecherous monster.
   I'd like to see him hang from an olive tree.

Enter COMMANDER, FLORES *and* ORTUÑO.

COMMANDER.
   My good people, God be with you.

ALONSO.
  Good, my lord!

COMMANDER.
                I'd like you all to sit down.

ALONSO.
  Will it please you, my lord, to sit
  In your accustomed place? We are
  Happy to stand, that's as it should be.

COMMANDER.
  I would like you all to sit down.

ESTEBAN.
  And we would like to stand, my lord:
  A sign of honour and respect,
  Honour is given to good men:
  Those without it can't give it.

COMMANDER.
  Sit down! We have things to discuss.

ESTEBAN.
  My lord, have you seen the greyhound
  We sent to your home?

COMMANDER.
                No, Mayor,
  But my men were most impressed.
  They tell me he runs like the wind.

ESTEBAN.
  He is an outstanding creature.
  I swear that beast can run faster
  Than a criminal from the law,
  Or a coward from a battle.

COMMANDER.
In this particular instance
I'd like you to set this hound to
Catch me a hare, one that is
Constantly avoiding my grasp.

ESTEBAN.
Where will I seek this creature, sir?

COMMANDER.
At home. I speak of your daughter.

ESTEBAN.
My daughter?

COMMANDER.
Yes.

ESTEBAN.
But, good my lord,
Is it right to hunt my daughter?

COMMANDER.
Mayor, give the girl some guidance.

ESTEBAN.
Why?

COMMANDER.
She seems determined to resist me.
To think there's a man in this square
Whose wife, at my very first glance,
Beat a path to my door.

ESTEBAN.
Then she did wrong.
And you do wrong, my lord, to speak
Of such matters with such licence!

COMMANDER.

An eloquent peasant! Flores,
Go to my study and bring us
Aristotle's *The Politics*.
I think the Mayor should read it.

ESTEBAN.

This town is happy to live under
Your honourable protection.
Remember, there are people of
Consequence in Fuente Ovejuna!

LEONELO (*aside*).

How dare he treat us with such contempt?

COMMANDER.

You, Deputy Mayor of the dunghill,
Did I say something to upset you?

ALONSO.

Your behavior is unreasonable,
What you have said here is unjust.
You should not insult our honour!

COMMANDER.

Do farmers claim to have honour?
Are you Knights of Calatrava?

ALONSO.

There may be those who wear the cross,
Whose blood is less pure than ours.

COMMANDER.

Are you suggesting that your blood
Would be sullied if mixed with mine?

ALONSO.
Bad actions leave a stain, my lord.

COMMANDER.
Someone had better tell your wives:
They have no fear of mingling blood.

ALONSO.
Your words insult our women.
Your actions are unforgivable!

COMMANDER.
What a dreary bunch of peasants.
Oh, thank God for the big cities
Where a man of taste and style
Can enjoy himself without censure.
Where husbands are pleased, even proud,
When a wife finds a guest for her bed.

ESTEBAN.
I don't believe that to be true.
You're trying to put us off our guard.
God's commandments still exist,
Even in big cities, as does
Jealousy and retribution!

COMMANDER.
Go home!

ALONSO.
          Sir, I would like to say:
I agree with everything he said.

COMMANDER.
You. Peasants. It's time to go home.
All of you. Move! Clear the square. Now!

ESTEBAN.
    We're leaving.

COMMANDER.
                    Yes! But not in gangs!

FLORES.
    Take it easy, sir, please, calm down!

COMMANDER.
    They are walking off in huddles.
    To hatch their plots behind closed doors!

ORTUÑO.
    You might show a bit of patience.

COMMANDER.
    I have shown too much already!
    You. Rustic scum! Leave the square. Now!
    Go back to your homes. One by one!

ESTEBAN.
    I'm leaving. In this direction.

LEONELO (*aside*).
    Heaven, will you let this happen?

Exit all but COMMANDER, FLORES *and* ORTUÑO.

COMMANDER.
    What do you think of these people?

ORTUÑO.
    You don't do much to hide the fact
    You don't give a damn about them,
    Their feelings, or their complaints.

COMMANDER.
They seem to think they're my equals.

FLORES.
I'm not sure that's the problem, sir.

COMMANDER.
And that lout who stole my crossbow,
Is he to remain unpunished?

FLORES.
Last night, I saw a man I thought
Was him, loitering right outside
Laurencia's front door, he was
Wearing the same kind of short cloak,
So I put a smile across his neck:
Slashed him from ear to ear: He fell,
I turned him over and, my God,
Turns out it wasn't him at all.

COMMANDER.
Where is this Frondoso hiding?

FLORES.
Rumour has it he's still hereabouts.

COMMANDER.
The scum who tried to kill me dares
To remain in my territory?

FLORES.
Don't worry, sir, we'll catch him soon,
Like an innocent bird in a snare
Or a gullible fish on a hook.

COMMANDER.

They say that when I raise my sword
The kingdom of Granada shakes,
Yet this peasant boy dares to point
My bow, directly at my heart.
Flores, what's happening to this world?

FLORES.

It's the power of love, sir.
And you're still here, alive and well.
I think that shows he respects you.

COMMANDER.

I've not yet shown what I feel.
If I had, within an hour of that
Incident, I'd have driven my sword
Deep into the heart of this dull
Peasant town: I'm waiting, and when
The moment comes; I'll strike, 'til then
I'm cooling my rage with reason.
What news of Pascuala?

FLORES.

               She said:
As she got engaged last week a date
Might be hard to arrange right now.

COMMANDER.

Trying to fob me off on credit?

FLORES.

Sending you to another till,
Where you might get paid in cash.

COMMANDER.

And Marcella?

ORTUÑO.

> She makes me laugh.
What a woman!

COMMANDER.

> And what a tongue!
What's her excuse?

ORTUÑO.

> She just got married
And as her hubby found your love note
On his pillow on their wedding night,
And as you keep standing under
Her balcony singing love songs:
The little tyrant's getting jealous.

COMMANDER.

On my sacred oath of Knighthood:
That little man misses nothing.

ORTUÑO.

Misses nothing, loves his missus.
When he calms down she'll let you in,
As she's done so many times before.

COMMANDER.

And Innes?

FLORES.

> Which Innes?

COMMANDER.

> Anton's wife.

FLORES.

She is happy to receive you

Whenever you want to see her.
We talked last night at her back door,
Which is your way in she tells me.

COMMANDER.

Easy women, don't you love them?
Use them often, pay them nothing.
Thank God the poor creatures don't know
How valuable they are to us.

FLORES.

There's nothing more disappointing
Than a girl who yields without a fight.
A quick surrender deprives us of
The pleasure of anticipation.
I know some women need a man
Like a desert needs rain but, come on,
I prefer some kind of challenge.

COMMANDER.

The man who is crazed with desire
Is delighted to have his passion
Quickly and easily fulfilled,
Although he then despises
The object of his affection:
The most romantic lover soon forgets
The women who cost him nothing!

Enter CIMBRANOS, *a soldier.*

CIMBRANOS.

Is Commander Gómez with you?

ORTUÑO.

Why ask? He's sitting over there.

CIMBRANOS.

    Fernán Gómez, our fearless leader:
    Swap your soft cloak for shining armour
    And exchange your green hunting cap
    For the white-plumed helmet of war.
    In the name of Ferdinand and Isabel,
    The Grand Master of Santiago
    And the valiant count of Cabra
    Have laid siege to Ciudad Real.
    Don Rodrigo calls out to you for support.
    Come now, or what Calatrava won
    At the cost of so much toil and blood
    Will be retaken by our enemies.
    I stood on the high battlement at dawn
    And by the light of the beacons I saw
    The massed forces of Castile and Leon:
    As strong as castles and as brave as lions.
    And though the King of Portugal has heaped
    All kinds of honours on his young shoulders
    I believe Rodrigo will be lucky
    To return to Almagro with his life.
    My lord, you must mount your horse and ride out
    The merest glimpse of you will be enough
    To put new heart into our men and send
    Our enemies running home to Castile.

COMMANDER.

    Cimbranos. Enough. Get ready.
    Ortuño, call the bugler:
    Order him to summon the men.
    How many do I have?

ORTUÑO.

                  Fifty-three, sir.

COMMANDER.
Tell them to prepare for battle.

CIMBRANOS.
If you don't leave now, I'm afraid
Ferdinand will retake the city.

COMMANDER.
He won't. That won't happen, soldier.

Exit all.

Scene Two

A wooded glade outside Fuente Ovejuna.

Enter MENGO, LAURENCIA *and* PASCUALA, *running, with torches.*

PASCUALA.
Mengo, you can't leave us alone!

MENGO.
Surely you're not frightened out here?

LAURENCIA.
Please, stay with us until we're home.
We don't walk in town now unless
We're in a group or with a man:
We're afraid of meeting him alone.

MENGO.
He's the devil and he's ripping
The heart out of our little world!

LAURENCIA.

    Day or night I never feel safe.

MENGO.

    In my prayers I ask God to send
    A firebolt to kill that madman!

LAURENCIA.

    More a monster than a madman
    Crushing the soul out of our village.

MENGO.

    People say that in the forest here
    Frondoso picked up his crossbow
    And aimed a bolt straight at his heart
    So that you could escape unharmed.

LAURENCIA.

    Before that, Mengo, I didn't
    Think much of, but Frondoso
    Was prepared to give his life to
    Save mine, and since then, well,
    I have to say, I've changed my mind.
    But, if the Commander's men catch him
    They will kill him for his kindness.

MENGO.

    If you see him tell him to run
    A thousand miles away from here.

LAURENCIA.

    I do see him, and though it hurts,
    I give him exactly that advice –
    Which makes him laugh in my face
    Then shout at me and curse me hard –

Although he knows full well Guzmán
Has sworn to hang him from a tree.

PASCUALA.
I wish Guzmán a painful death!

MENGO.
An old-style stoning would be best.
Look, you see this simple sling?
I use it to protect my sheep.
Well, I swear before God above
If I could get one good shot at him
They'd hear his skull crack wide open
All the way down to the coast, y'know
That vicious Roman general
Lucius Julius Brutilicus?

LAURENCIA.
I'm sorry, Mengo, do you mean:
Lucius Junius Brutus?
The founder of Rome?

MENGO.
                    Well, I'm not
A trained historian, in fact
I'm not sure what day of the week
It is, but yeah, well, you know:
Lucius, jumping jack, brutal boy,
The Roman guy, he had nothing
On Guzmán; come on, did nature
Ever make a monster like him?

PASCUALA.
No: he has the soul of a tigress!

Enter JACINTA.

JACINTA.

> In the name of Heaven, help me,
> Help me, please, help, my dear friends.

LAURENCIA.

> Jacinta, we'll help you, what's wrong?

PASCUALA.

> We are your friends; we're here to help.

JACINTA.

> Guzmán is leaving town tonight
> Marching to defend Ciudad Real.
> Two of his men knocked on my door
> Armed, not with honest courage
> But with brutal lust, and tried to
> Drag me away with him to war.

LAURENCIA.

> Jacinta, Heaven must help you,
> I can't. If he'll treat you like this
> Think what he's planning for me!

> *Exit* LAURENCIA.

PASCUALA.

> Jacinta, friend, what use am I?
> You need a man to protect you.

> *Exit* PASCUALA.

MENGO.

> Oh no, it's all down to me then.
> A man, well, that's what they call me.
> Cousin, come on, I'll protect you.

JACINTA.

> Do you have a weapon?

MENGO.

Of course!

The first weapon!

JACINTA.

What do you mean?

MENGO.

A stone, look, a stone and a sling.

Enter FLORES *and* ORTUÑO.

FLORES.

Trying to run away, pretty one?

JACINTA.

Mengo, this is it!

MENGO.

Gentlemen!

Why do you hunt such humble game?

ORTUÑO.

Are you man enough to defend
This little damsel in distress?

MENGO.

First, I'll protect her with a plea:
My masters, please, don't harm this girl.
She's my cousin, I must defend her.

FLORES.

Kill him; we don't have time for this.

MENGO.

By God, don't make me lose my temper.
If I take this sling from my belt
You'll be sorry you provoked me.

Enter the COMMANDER, CIMBRANOS *and other*
SOLDIERS.

COMMANDER.
What is going on here? Do I
Have to dismount to deal with this?

FLORES.
The people of this ugly town,
Which you should burn to the ground
As they give you nothing but grief,
Are once again defying your orders.

MENGO.
Lord, if pity lives in your heart
Or a sense of what's right and just,
You will punish these two men who
Have tried to abduct this woman
From her husband and her parents.
Let me escort this poor girl home.
I beg you, give me permission.

COMMANDER.
I'd rather give them permission
To cut out your yapping tongue.
Drop that weapon, peasant.

MENGO.
                  My lord!

COMMANDER.
Flores, Ortuño, Cimbranos.
Grab him and bind his hands with his sling.

MENGO.
Is this how you defend her honour?

COMMANDER.
    And who do the rustic rabble of
    Fuente Ovejuna think I am?

MENGO.
    Listen, sir, how have I, how has our
    Community offended you?

FLORES.
    Shall I kill him?

COMMANDER.
                        Don't stain your blade.
    You are soon to honour it in
    Another more important place.

ORTUÑO.
    What shall we do with him?

COMMANDER.
                                    Whip him.

MENGO.
    Mercy! As you are a man of honour.

COMMANDER.
    Strip his dirty rags, bind his hands,
    Tie him to a tree and whip him
    Until the buckles of your belts
    Turn his backside black and blue.

MENGO.
    Heaven, you see what they're doing?
    When will you punish these crimes?

    Exit MENGO, FLORES *and* ORTUÑO.

COMMANDER.

My little one, why run away?
Do you reject an aristocrat
In favor of a boorish peasant?

JACINTA.

Your men tried to take my honour,
Is this how you punish their crime,
By stealing it yourself?

COMMANDER.

Stealing?

JACINTA.

Sir, be careful, I have a father
Who, though not a man of your rank,
Lives a good, simple, honest life,
A man who would die defending
His daughter's honour.

COMMANDER.

Do you think
Boring me with this dreary blather
Is the way to cool my desire?
Come here, my girl.

JACINTA.

Why would I?

COMMANDER.

To be closer.

JACINTA.

Think what you're doing.

COMMANDER.

I've thought and you'll wish I hadn't.

I won't have you, ungrateful slut
You'll be the battalion's whore!

JACINTA.
While I can still take my own life
No man has power over me.

COMMANDER.
Get moving, we're in a hurry.

JACINTA.
Sir, show mercy.

COMMANDER.
I have none.

JACINTA.
Heaven watches all our actions.
Soon you will suffer its judgement!

JACINTA is seized and dragged away.

Exit all.

Scene Three

Outside the home of ESTEBAN.

Enter FRONDOSO *and* LAURENCIA.

LAURENCIA.
Frondoso: you are such a fool!
Why come into town?

FRONDOSO.
To help you
Appreciate how much and how

Hopelessly you're in love with me!
From the hills I saw Guzmán leave
Which banished all my fears and
Expecting the warmest welcome
I ran down here to be with you.
I hope that madman never returns
From his battle!

LAURENCIA.

         Don't curse him!
Remember what the old folk say:
Those we most wish dead live longest.

FRONDOSO.

If that's what they say, I wish him
A thousand happy years and pray
That my good wishes end his days.
Laurencia, I've come here to know
If your resistance has melted.
The whole town sees us as one,
The whole town is surprised that we
Haven't yet walked up the aisle.
Can you swallow your pride and say
What it is to be, yes or no?

LAURENCIA.

I'll tell you, as I'll tell the town:
Yes. I accept your proposal.

FRONDOSO.

Let me kiss your beautiful feet
For the gift you have given me.
Laurencia, what can I say?
You've given me my life again.

LAURENCIA.

Let's not waste time with compliments.
And before we go any further
You have to talk to my father.
I won't marry without his consent.
Look, he's coming with my uncle:
Frondoso, chin up, get his blessing
And I will be your wife.

FRONDOSO.

Please, God.

LAURENCIA *conceals herself.*

Enter ESTEBAN *and* ALONSO.

ESTEBAN.

No one in that square tonight
Could believe what was happening.
His behaviour was irrational,
Quite beyond the bounds of reason.
The town is in a state of shock,
Terrified of what he'll do next.
And what about poor Jacinta:
Do you think we'll see her again?

ALONSO.

One day all the people of Spain
Will live under the jurisdiction
Of Ferdinand and Isabella.
They'll establish the rule of law.
My heart goes out to her family;
She was a good wife and daughter.

ESTEBAN.

And Mengo whipped?

ALONSO.

As he tried
To protect her: he was beaten
Every shade of black and blue.

ESTEBAN.

My friend, don't tell me any more.
It makes me shake with rage to hear
Of these terrible crimes while I
Hold this ancient staff of office,
Powerless to help my people.

ALONSO.

He's gone now, soon to be defeated.

ESTEBAN.

There have been other outrages.
Pedro Redondo spoke to me:
A week ago at the far end
Of the meadow, Guzmán ambushed
His wife and after he'd abused her
He handed her on to his men.

ALONSO.

Stand back. Who's there?

FRONDOSO.

Only me.
Waiting for permission to speak.

ESTEBAN.

Frondoso, outside my house
You don't need permission to speak.
Your dear father gave you life
But you've been like a son to me.

I've watched you grow from child to man.
No one could love you more than I.

FRONDOSO.
Knowing that love, I have come here,
To ask for a special favour.
Trusting in the love that you
Have always shown to me,
And sure of Laurencia's love,
I've come to ask for her hand.
I know, perhaps, I've spoken too soon.
Because this is so important
I think, my words got ahead of me.
Perhaps someone else should have asked.

ESTEBAN.
My boy, your request is timely.
You've given me another ten years
Of life and cured an ache in my heart
That I thought might never be eased.
I thank you for this proposal.
You bring honour to my house.
I thank God for your honest love.
But it wouldn't be right to proceed
Without your father's consent, so
Let us say I approve, pending
Your father's acceptance. I will
Be the luckiest man alive
If we can make this marriage work.

ALONSO.
You'd better get the girl's consent
Before you speak to his father.

ESTEBAN.
>Laurencia must have agreed:
>He wouldn't ask unless she had.
>These days they arrange it all
>Themselves; fathers, the last to know.
>Son, I wonder if you're concerned
>About the dowry; if so, stop.
>I want to give you a good start.

FRONDOSO.
>I really don't need a dowry.
>Keep your money in your pocket.

ALONSO.
>He will take her as God made her.
>You ought to thank your lucky stars.

ESTEBAN.
>Let's not assume Laurencia
>Will agree with this. Shall I ask?

FRONDOSO.
>Assumption is the mother of
>Many mistakes, sir. Please, ask her.

ESTEBAN.
>Laurencia! Daughter!

LAURENCIA.
>   Father.

ESTEBAN.
>I call and she comes in a flash:
>I told you she was in on this.
>My daughter, dear Laurencia,
>I must have a word, in private.

Would you step this way with me?
It's time Frondoso was married.
He's an honourable young man.
What would you say if he was
Married to your best friend, Blanca?

LAURENCIA.
What does Blanca say?

ESTEBAN.

                   She's a good catch,
A worthy match for him I think.

LAURENCIA.
I agree. Let them be married.

ESTEBAN.
Yes, but don't be hasty daughter.
Isn't she a little ugly?
Shouldn't he be asking for you?

LAURENCIA.
Please, stop playing these awful jokes.

ESTEBAN.
Do you love him?

LAURENCIA.

               He has feelings:
I have feelings. It's what we want.

ESTEBAN.
You want me to give my blessing?

LAURENCIA.
Yes, but only if you approve.

ESTEBAN.

Me, what have I to do with this?
Gentlemen, we are both agreed.
But we must talk to your father.
Shall we go and knock on his door?

ALONSO.

Come along. It's late!

ESTEBAN.

                    Frondoso.
Son. The dowry. What would you say
If I was to offer your father
Four thousand maravedis?

FRONDOSO.

With respect, don't ask the question.
I won't take any money from you.

ESTEBAN.

You say that now and you mean it
But those feelings won't last for ever.
One morning you'll wake up wondering:
'Why didn't I take the dowry?'

Exit ALONSO *and* ESTEBAN.

LAURENCIA.

Frondoso, are you happy now?

FRONDOSO.

I don't know why my heart hasn't
Burst with pride and why my head
Is still sitting on my shoulders:
That's how happy you've made me.
And these tears, are tears of joy

I am laughing through my eyes,
It's so hard to believe you're mine.

Exit all.

Scene Four

Outside the walls of Ciudad Real.

Enter COMMANDER, MASTER, FLORES, ORTUÑO,
CIMBRANOS *and* SOLDIERS.

COMMANDER.
Master! Retreat! Quickly! Run! Escape! Run! This way!

MASTER.
The wall of the city was weak! It just collapsed.
King Ferdinand's forces were too strong for us.

COMMANDER.
They lost a lot of men. That battle cost them blood.

MASTER.
But they can't boast they got their hands on our colours.
They will never take the cross of Calatrava.

COMMANDER.
Master, all your dreams of glory have been destroyed.

MASTER.
What could I have done? Fortune is a cruel goddess
One day she lifts us, the next she casts us in the dirt.

SHOUTS (*off*).
All hail the victors, Ferdinand and Isabella.
All hail the victors, the monarchs of Castile.

MASTER.

They're crowning each battlement with a flaming torch.
Draping banners from the windows of every tower.

COMMANDER.

The blood of their dead is dripping from those banners.
This is a moment for grief not celebration.

MASTER.

Fernán Gómez, I will return to Almagro.

COMMANDER.

And I to Fuente Ovejuna. You will have to decide
Whether to continue to support your kinsman
Or transfer your allegiance to the Catholic Kings.

MASTER.

I will write to you when I've made up my mind.

COMMANDER.

Time will show you the true path.

MASTER.

                        I'm sure it will!
When we're green, what do we know? Nothing! I'll learn!

Exit all.

Scene Five

The town square in Fuente Ovejuna.

Enter LAURENCIA, FRONDOSO *and the* CITIZENS *of Fuente Ovejuna, in wedding attire.*

SONG: *'Viva Laurencia'*

Viva Laurencia!
Viva Frondoso!
Vivan muchos años,
Los desposados.
Vivan muchos años!
Viva Laurencia!
Viva Frondoso!
A good life and a long life!
She's gonna make a good wife!
Vivan muchos años.

Viva Laurencia!
Viva Frondoso!
A good life and a long life!
She's gonna make a good wife!
Vivan muchos años!
Vivan muchos años!

MENGO.
    You didn't lose a lot of sleep
    Making up the words to that one!

BARRILDO.
    I suppose you could do better?

FRONDOSO.
    Mengo has taken a good whipping
    But can he whip words into lyrics?

MENGO.
    There was a man in a meadow
    Who picked up a Commander's bow.

BARRILDO.
    Don't name that murdering tyrant.
    That monster dishonours us all.

MENGO.

And think what his men did to me.
One shepherd and his sling against
A hundred mercenary killers.
I was lucky, think of the poor guy
Who was given an enema!
I won't mention his name but he's known
To all here as an honourable man,
An enema of ink and gravel!
How could anyone stand for that?

BARRILDO.

Perhaps Gómez found it amusing.

MENGO.

Enemas might keep you healthy
But since when were they amusing?

ALONSO.

Time to listen to Barrildo's dedication.

BARRILDO.

Let angels bless this man and wife,
Their days be free of rows and strife,
Their barns be full of golden wheat,
A dozen children grace their feet.
And on the day they pass away,
I hope that they can truly say:
'I'm glad I took this precious ring,
I wouldn't change a single thing.'

ALL.

Laurencia and Frondoso!

MENGO.

Well, that put the dog in doggerel.

BARRILDO.

   It was written rather quickly!

MENGO.

   Here's something I made up last night.
   This puts poets in their places.

SONG: 'The Poet in His Study'

   Have you seen a doughnut maker
   Working at his pastry dough?
   Chucking lumps in boiling oil
   'Til his pan is full to go?

   Most come out all fat and soggy.
   And a few fry up just fine,
   Most are burnt and so misshapen,
   Cooking was a waste of time.

   It's like the poet in his study
   As he sits and has a go,
   Tugging at his sticky verses,
   Like the baker and his dough.

   The poet puts his verse on paper:
   And the paper is his plate,
   He dusts it all in rhyming sugar,
   To hide mistakes but much too late.

   It's like the poet in his study
   As he sits and has a go,
   Tugging at his sticky verses,
   Like the baker and his dough.

   Both men travel off to market,
   Selling poems and doughnuts,
   No surprise, when they sell nothing,
   And both of them get swollen guts.

Cos the poet eats his unsold verses,
He's nothing left as market shuts,
And as the baker's starving hungry,
He must sup on stale doughnuts.

BARRILDO.
Songwriters all over the world
Are grinding their teeth into dust.

ALONSO.
Now it's time to bless the bride and groom.

LAURENCIA.
Father-in-law, will you bless us?

JUAN ROJO.
Laurencia, you ask my blessing?
You should first ask for your father's,
After all he's done for you both.

ESTEBAN.
Friend, I hope Heaven blesses them
And offers them a helping hand.

FRONDOSO.
Father-in-law, Father, why don't
You do the blessing together?

BLESSING (*sung*).
Ave Maria, gratia plena
Sancta Maria, Mater Dei
Ora pro nobis peccatoribus
Nunc et in hora mortis nostrae.

BARRILDO.
Now the blessings are over,
Laurencia and Frondoso,

With your permission, we give you:
'The Tale of the Fair Young Maiden.'
Musicians, ready? Actors begin!

A dumb show with music and song.

MUSICIANS (*singing*).
Through the forest runs
The maid with golden hair.
Chased by a man on whose breast,
A cross of crimson burns there.

She seeks a hiding place,
Ashamed and confused.
Sheltering in a bush,
Courage she must use.

'Oh, why do you run away?
And, maid, where will you go?
For I am a man in love,
And I will never say no!'

The knight, he comes so close,
The maid, she's afraid to breathe,
Shaking in her shelter,
Of branches, thorns and leaves.

'Maid, you will never escape me,
For I'll climb every hill
And I'll cut down every tree,
Hide wherever you will.'

'Oh, why do you run away?
And, maid, where will you go?
For I am a man in love,
And I will never say no!'

Enter COMMANDER, FLORES, ORTUÑO,
CIMBRANOS *and* SOLDIERS.

COMMANDER.
    What's here? A wedding. In your seats!
    Calm down, there will be no trouble.

JUAN ROJO.
    This is a sacred day, my lord!
    Perhaps you would care to join us?
    May I offer you a seat, a drink?
    Why come here dressed for battle?
    I assume you were victorious?
    Oh, perhaps I said something wrong?

FRONDOSO (*aside*).
    Help, Heaven! I'm as good as dead.

LAURENCIA (*aside*).
    Frondoso! Run!

COMMANDER.
                    Stop him! Hold him!
    Bind his hands!

JUAN ROJO.
                    Son, let them arrest you!

FRONDOSO.
    But Father, they will kill me!

JUAN ROJO.
    What crime have you committed?

COMMANDER.
    Only the most brutal tyrant
    Would condemn a man to death

Without giving him a fair trial.
And were I that kind of monster
My men would have murdered this man
A long time ago: Flores,
Arrest him, take him to prison.
His own father will be his judge
When he stands trial for his crimes.

PASCUALA.
My lord, this is his wedding day.

COMMANDER.
That is no concern of the law.
The village is full of young men,
Let the bride choose another.

PASCUALA.
                                            Sir!
If he's offended, forgive him,
Show the world your compassion.

COMMANDER.
Pascuala, I'm not offended.
His deeds have sullied the honour
Of the Order of Calatrava.
He's offended the Grand Master
Rodrigo Girón, God protect him,
And he must pay, justice must be
Seen to be done. Not to deal with
This crime might inspire other
Insurgents to rebellion:
He stole a crossbow and aimed it
At the heart of a High Commander.
Can such an insult be ignored?

ESTEBAN.

    Sir, as the boy's father-in-law,
    May I offer up an excuse?
    He's a young man and he's in love.
    In the circumstances, can we
    Be surprised at his behaviour?
    Sir, he saw you attempting to
    Deprive him of his young wife,
    Is it not natural for him
    To try and defend his sweetheart?

COMMANDER.

    Mayor, you're not making sense.

ESTEBAN.

    I appeal to your better self.

COMMANDER.

    How could I deprive him of his wife?
    The boy's only just got married.

ESTEBAN.

    You know what happened! That's enough.
    There are monarchs in Castile
    Who'll establish the rule of law
    And wipe away this anarchy.
    When they have some respite from war
    They will do well to rid their towns
    And villages of men like you,
    Who terrorise the people and who
    Seem to believe they can behave
    With impunity because they wear
    A holy red cross on their chest.
    Only a king should bear that mark,
    It's an emblem for a royal breast.

COMMANDER.

Ortuño. Give me the Mayor's staff.

ESTEBAN.

My lord, please take it and welcome.

COMMANDER.

I will break this across your back
As if you were a stubborn old donkey.

ESTEBAN.

You are my master. I must obey.

PASCUALA.

You'll beat an innocent old man?

LAURENCIA.

You're beating him to punish me.
And what crime have I committed?

COMMANDER.

Seize her! Bind her! And lock her up!
I want her guarded by ten men.

Exit COMMANDER *and* SOLDIERS, *with* LAURENCIA *and* FRONDOSO.

ESTEBAN.

Heaven, we await your justice.

Exit ESTEBAN.

PASCUALA.

It was a wedding, now it's a wake.

Exit PASCUALA.

BARRILDO.

Friends, who'll make a stand with me?

MENGO.

    I stood up and I got knocked down.
    Oppose him and he'll have you whipped.

JUAN ROJO.

    We must meet up and talk.

MENGO.

                       Not me!
    If you want my advice, go home.
    Keep your heads down and say nothing.
    His men beat me so hard, my arse
    Looks like a pair of raw salmon steaks.

Exit all.

End of Act Two.

ACT THREE

Scene One

A meeting room in the town hall in Fuente Ovejuna.

ESTEBAN.
Can we begin?

BARRILDO.
We're still waiting on some people.

ESTEBAN.
Every minute we lose moves us closer to disaster.

BARRILDO.
Everyone's been told the last few are on their way.

ESTEBAN.
Frondoso arrested and facing execution,
Laurencia abducted, facing God knows what.
Merciful Heaven! You have to find a way to . . .

Enter JUAN ROJO *and a* COUNCILLOR.

JUAN ROJO.
Esteban. Stop shouting. You can be heard outside.
This meeting must be secret. We all depend on that.

ESTEBAN.
It's a miracle I don't shout any louder.

Enter MENGO.

MENGO.

> I decided to come, let the meeting begin.

ESTEBAN.

> Honourable farmers and friends, I stand before you
> An old man whose white beard is wet with tears,
> To ask what funeral rites can be spoken
> Over the rotting corpse of our once dear town?
> Such sacred words demand an honourable voice
> And who amongst us can still lay claim to that?
> Is there a man in this room whose dignity has
> Escaped unscathed? Look around you, council members.
> ·There is no one here that man has not disgraced.
> We share the same suffering, the same enemy.
> We have endured enough: what have we left to fear?

JUAN ROJO.

> We have endured the worst crimes imaginable.
> However, I've received news that Ferdinand and
> Isabella, having secured peace in Castile,
> Are making their way south: I propose that we send
> Two council members to meet them in Córdoba
> To fall at their feet and to beg them for justice!

BARRILDO.

> But Ferdinand and Isabella are fighting
> Many battles on many fronts; they won't have time
> To deal with our troubles. With the greatest respect,
> I think we should try to find another solution.

LEONELO.

> If anyone would like to hear my opinion
> I vote that we evacuate the town. Tonight!

JUAN ROJO.

> Not practical! Evacuation would take days!

MENGO.

> If the Commander finds out we're up to something
> Like that, he will kill every last man in this room.

ALONSO.

> My friends, the mast of our little ship is broken
> And we are sailing in a dangerous sea
> Beyond thoughts of tolerance, restraint or fear.
> With brutal violence he abducted the daughter
> Of the good man who governs our community,
> And across his honest back with no sense of shame
> We saw him break the ancient staff of office!
> What slave was ever treated with such vile contempt?

JUAN ROJO.

> But what do you advise? What can the people do?

ALONSO.

> We lie down and die or kill those who abuse us.
> There are so few of them and so many of us.

BARRILDO.

> You mean take up arms against our sovereign lord?

ESTEBAN.

> In the eyes of God only the King is sovereign.
> We owe no loyalty to men who behave like
> Wild animals, and if Heaven supports our cause
> What have we to fear?

MENGO.

>   Gentlemen, it's important
> We proceed from here with all possible caution.
> I represent the peasants, perhaps the poorest
> Members of our community, who I fear would
> Suffer the most should we follow your proposal.

JUAN ROJO.
>   What is left to fear? Our lives are being destroyed!
>   His men are burning down our homes and our vineyards!
>   He is a tyrant! It is time to take revenge.

Enter LAURENCIA, *dishevelled.*

LAURENCIA.
>   Let me in, open the door.
>   I want to address this meeting,
>   Though I'm not allowed to vote here,
>   I have the right to plead my case.
>   Do you recognise me?

ESTEBAN.
>   God, help us!
>   Is that my daughter?

JUAN ROJO.
>   There she is.
>   Laurencia!

LAURENCIA.
>   Yes, it's me:
>   In such a state that you don't know me.

ESTEBAN.
>   Daughter!

LAURENCIA.
>   No! Don't call me that!
>   Not 'daughter'.

ESTEBAN.
>   Why, my precious one?
>   Why not that?

LAURENCIA.
                    I have my reasons.
Let's begin with the obvious.
You stood and watched as I was snatched,
Abducted on my wedding day,
Watched, without lifting a finger,
When protecting me was clearly
Your responsibility: your job
To fight for me, you failed: your job
To take revenge, you let me down.
Before the wedding night it's the
Father, not the husband, who should
Protect the women of his house:
When you buy a diamond ring
You're not liable for its safety,
Not for you to fight off criminals
Not until it's safe at home.
You watched his thugs seize me and
Drag me to his lair like a
Frightened shepherd watches a wolf
Run off with a lamb in its jaws.
They held their weapons to my throat,
Whispered obscenities in my ears,
Used every kind of cunning trick
To make me yield my body up
To his vile, insatiable lust!
Does my hair tell you a story?
The scratches on my neck and chest?
The bruises on my thighs? The blood?
And you call yourselves good fathers?
And you call yourselves decent men?
Your hearts should burst wide open

To see one of your own like this!
Fuente Ovejuna! That's us.
The spring of fresh water for sheep,
And how appropriate the name
When timid lambs live here, not men!
You blocks of stone, cold-hearted as
The tigress: no, not the tigress,
For she ferociously chases down
The hunters who steal her children,
Killing them without mercy before
Throwing herself into the sea:
So, not tigresses, no, but rabbits!
Hiding in your little holes: you
Roosters strutting on a dunghill
While other men violate your wives.
Why do those swords hang at your sides?
Why don't I lend you my knitting
Needles to stick into your belts!
Then you can watch us do the job.
Women! We'll wipe away the stain,
Drink the blood of the abusers:
Then we will stone you in the streets,
You cowards! You eunuchs! You traitors!
We'll parade you about the town
Dressed in our Sunday best, a nice
Headscarf, a smart skirt, a dab of
Perfume and a smudge of rouge, so:
Listen. Up there, the Commander
Is going to hang Frondoso
Without any kind of charge,
Without any kind of trial,
Hang him from a tree in his yard

Then he'll come for you and I'll rejoice
As he empties this village of its
Gutless and impotent failures,
And we will replace you, a tribe
Of brave Amazonian women
Will restore dignity to this town
And our deeds will stagger the world.

ESTEBAN.
My daughter, I am not sitting here
To be called any more vile names.
It's time to fight and I'm going,
I'll go alone if I have to.
No matter what's decided here.

JUAN ROJO.
I'm with you! It is time to fight,
However strong our enemy.

ALONSO.
We fight as one! We die as one!

BARRILDO.
We march together, heads held high.

JUAN ROJO.
In what order shall we march?

MENGO.
We go now and kill him without
Thinking about marching order,
We're united, with one desire:
Yes? To kill those who abuse us!

ESTEBAN.
Arm yourselves with knives and daggers,
Swords and sickles, pikes and hammers!

MENGO.
  Long live the King and Queen!

ALL.

                                    Our true masters!

MENGO.
  And death to those who abuse us!

ALL.
  Those who abuse us must die!

  Exit all but LAURENCIA.

LAURENCIA.
  Go! Now! Fight! Heaven protect them.
  Women of Fuente Ovejuna.
  Hear me! Come! Come here! Come now!
  Come and reclaim your dignity.

  Enter PASCUALA, JACINTA *and other* WOMEN.

PASCUALA.
  Laurencia, what's going on?!

LAURENCIA.
  Come! Come and see our men running
  To destroy Guzmán and his thugs!
  Look, there, young men, old men and boys.
  Running to do what must be done.
  Now, let me ask you, is it right
  That only our men should enjoy
  The glory of this night? The abuse
  We've endured is no less than theirs.

JACINTA.
  What do you suggest we do?

LAURENCIA.
    Form ourselves into an army
    And do such things that the world
    Will never forget our names: Jacinta!
    The awful things you've suffered
    Will be our inspiration.
    You lead our brigade of women!

JACINTA.
    But they hurt you as much as me.

LAURENCIA.
    Pascuala! You be our standard bearer!

PASCUALA.
    I'll find a banner and a staff
    And carry our colours with pride.

LAURENCIA.
    Hoist a headscarf on a broomstick,
    No time for digging out banners,
    Fortune is smiling on us now,
    Let's grasp the moment while it's ours!

PASCUALA.
    Who'll be our Cid, our Rodomonte!

LAURENCIA.
    No one! Because when I'm on fire
    We need no hero from the past
    To lead us screaming into battle!

    Exit all.

Scene Two

The residence of the COMMANDER.

Enter FRONDOSO, *bound,* COMMANDER, FLORES, ORTUÑO *and* CIMBRANOS.

COMMANDER.
It's time to take him into the yard and hang him.
You can use the rope left over from binding his hands.
And disembowel him before you string him up.

FRONDOSO.
My lord, how will history judge your actions?

COMMANDER.
Hang him from the almond tree next to the wall.

FRONDOSO.
Sir, I never intended to fire that bolt.
I wasn't trying to kill you!

FLORES.
Stop! Listen.

COMMANDER.
What?

FLORES.
An angry mob are marching up here, coming
To stop the execution.

ORTUÑO.
They're ramming the gates!

COMMANDER.
This is a residence of the sacred order!
How dare they touch my gates?

FLORES.

The whole town's out there.

JUAN ROJO (*off*).
Knock them down! Tear them down! Smash! Destroy!
And burn!

ORTUÑO.
When a mob's fired up like that it's hard to contain.

COMMANDER.
My people, rise up against me?

FLORES.

They're on fire!
They've broken down your gates and they're running this
way.

COMMANDER.
You. Quickly. Untie his hands. And you.
Frondoso. Go and calm them. Talk to the Mayor.

FRONDOSO.
My lord, it is love that inspires them to do this.

Exit FRONDOSO.

MENGO (*off*).
Long live Ferdinand and Isabella, and death
To the traitors!

FLORES.

Sir, please, I am begging you!
Don't let that mob find you here.

COMMANDER.
There are soldiers out there.

If they try to enter this room they'll encounter
Very stern resistance.

FLORES.

           When a mob is raging
With such an insane passion it won't stop until
It gets what it came for, sir: that's blood and revenge!

COMMANDER.

Draw your swords. This threshold will be our portcullis.
We will cut out this ugly passion with our steel.

FRONDOSO (*off*).

Justice! For Fuente Ovejuna!

COMMANDER.

               The lout's turned, Captain!
I'll go and smash those words back down his peasant throat.

FLORES.

Your reckless words are filling me with terror, sir!

ESTEBAN (*off*).

Fuente Ovejuna! Kill Guzmán and his thugs!
Fuente Ovejuna! Now we kill the traitors!

Enter the MEN *of Fuente Ovejuna, armed.*

COMMANDER.

My people! Listen. Wait!

ALL.

              Our revenge cannot wait!

COMMANDER.

Let me hear every complaint against me. I swear
On my honour, I will resolve every grievance.

ALL.

    Fuente Ovejuna! Long live King Ferdinand!
    Death to the evil one! The traitors must die!

COMMANDER.

    You will listen to me! You will let me say my piece!
    I am your lord and master!

ALL.

                     Our true masters
    Are King Ferdinand and Queen Isabella!

COMMANDER.

    Wait!

ALL.

    Fuente Ovejuna! Death to the Commander!

Exit all.

Scene Three

Outside the COMMANDER*'s residence.*

Enter the WOMEN *of Fuente Ovejuna, armed.*

LAURENCIA.

    Stop here, women, soldiers, hungry for justice.
    Here is the place where our dreams will be fulfilled.

PASCUALA.

    Tyrant! Quake!

PEASANT WOMAN.

                Women have come to take revenge!

PASCUALA.
Let him come out here. Watch me spill his evil blood.

JACINTA.
Throw him from the window. We'll catch him on our
spears.

PASCUALA.
Come, throw him down, our spikes are hungry for his
flesh.

ESTEBAN (*off*).
Die! Commander! Tyrant! Abuser! Die!

COMMANDER (*off*).

I'm dead.
May God forgive me and have mercy on my soul.

BARRILDO (*off*).
Here comes that pimp Flores.

MENGO (*off*).

Let me at that bastard.
That vicious monster turned my backside black and blue.

FRONDOSO (*off*).
I want him. I'm going to rip out his rotten soul.

LAURENCIA.
Why are we holding back? Let's go inside!

PASCUALA.

But surely:
We should stay out here and guard the doors.

BARRILDO (*off*).

No mercy. None.
Now it's your turn to be afraid. Your turn to weep.

LAURENCIA.
    Pascuala, I'm going in. I can't wait any longer,
    I can't keep this sword sleeping in its scabbard.

    Exit LAURENCIA.

BARRILDO (*off*).
    Who's that? Here comes Ortuño.

FRONDOSO (*off*).

    Slash his ugly face!

    Enter FLORES *with* MENGO, *chasing.*

FLORES.
    Mengo, have mercy. I was following orders.

MENGO.
    You were the tyrant's pimp, for that you deserve to die!
    But then you whipped me! That's a second death
        sentence!

PASCUALA.
    Mengo, give him to us. Let us women have him.
    Lay off him, let him go!

MENGO.

    Pascuala, you're right, he's your prize.
    Who could punish him better? Take him and kill him.

PASCUALA.
    We'll avenge your beating!

JACINTA.

    Enough talk. Let's do it.

FLORES.
    Murdered by the hands of women?

JACINTA.
    But isn't that fitting?

PASCUALA.
                        Women's hands not good enough?

JACINTA.
    You organised his evil pleasures. Now you suffer.

PASCUALA.
    Pimp, prepare to die.

FLORES.
                        Mercy. Ladies. Forgive me.

    Enter ORTUÑO, *fleeing* LAURENCIA.

ORTUÑO.
    Please! I swear! It wasn't me!

LAURENCIA.
                        I know who you are!
    Women, time to go inside and dip your weapons
    In the tyrant's blood!

PASCUALA.
                        I'll gorge on that until I burst!

ALL.
    Fuente Ovejuna! Long live the Catholic Kings!

    Exit all.

Scene Four

The Court of the Catholic Kings in Toledo.

Enter DON MANRIQUE, KING FERDINAND, QUEEN ISABELLA *and* COURTIERS.

MANRIQUE.
 Your Majesty, all went to plan.
 Our strategy proved effective
 And our objectives were fulfilled
 Efficiently, with few losses.
 The forces of Calatrava
 Offered little resistance
 But had they offered more, our troops
 Would have risen to the challenge.
 The Count of Cabra has remained
 In the city as a precaution
 Against any counterattack
 Rodrigo might launch against us.

FERDINAND.
 A very prudent decision.
 We'll send Cabra reinforcements.
 He can supervise the rebuilding
 And maintain control of the pass.
 With a stronghold in Ciudad Real
 We've no reason to fear Portugal's
 Troops on our border. We can
 Block any advance from the west:
 I am sure the Count will govern
 The city with his customary
 Bravery and skill, defending
 Our victory and securing us
 Against future attack.

He'll be a vigilant watchman,
A sentinel for his country's good.

Enter FLORES, *wounded.*

FLORES.
Ferdinand, great Catholic King,
To whom Heaven in its wisdom
Has given the Crown of Castile:
I come to report the worst crime
Ever witnessed by the eyes of man
In any land visited by the sun!

FERDINAND.
Soldier. Calm yourself.

FLORES.
              My lord
I'm wounded and my time is short,
Let me report what has happened
Quickly: while I can still draw breath.
I come from Fuente Ovejuna
Where the mutinous subjects
Of that rebellious town have,
Without right and without mercy,
Murdered their feudal lord.
Fernán Gómez is dead, slaughtered
In his own home by a savage mob.
Serfs who have a mind to feel wronged
Revolt with little provocation.
They called him tyrant and with that
Harsh and unproven accusation
Their only justification,
They committed their hideous crime.

They smashed down his gates, he swore
On his sacred honour as a knight
To listen to all their complaints
But they were deaf to all his words
And a multitude of cruel blades
Carved holes in the cross on his breast.
His corpse was thrown from a window
Onto the points of spikes and spears
Held by a mob of women below,
Who dragged his body to a barn
Where, crying with rage and delight,
They fought each other for the right
To rip the beard clean off his face.
They smashed his teeth with the pommel
Of his own sword, and they hacked
At his corpse with such bestial
Spite that the largest parts of him
That remained were his ears.
His coat of arms was stamped in the
Dirt and they bellowed allegiance
To you and your Queen, promising
To raise your flag, announcing that
All these deeds were done in your name.
They ransacked his home as if
Plundering some fallen city,
Sharing jokes as they debated
Who should take the richest pickings.
I saw all this from the hiding place
Where malevolent fate decreed
I should watch but not share my master's
Tragic exit from this harsh world.
I lay in that ditch all day, waiting

For darkness so I might escape
And come here to give you an honest
Account of these terrible events.
Your Majesty, you're a good king.
Let the world now witness your justice.
My master's blood cries out for revenge,
Let these cruel monsters feel the full force
Of a just king's retribution!

FERDINAND.
Captain, you may rest assured
These crimes will not go unpunished.
What you have told us is without
Precedent and I am amazed.
We will send a magistrate to
Confirm this soldier's report
And arrest all guilty parties.
This crime must be seen to receive
The punishment that it deserves.
We'll send a captain with the judge,
The town might still be dangerous.
Let this soldier's wounds be looked to.

Exit all.

Scene Five

The town square in Fuente Ovejuna.

The head of the COMMANDER *is fixed on a pole. Enter*
CITIZENS *of Fuente Ovejuna, bloodsoaked and singing*

CITIZENS (*singing*).
Victory to our King and Queen

Isabel y Fernando,
And death to the abusers.
Muchos años vivan
Isabel y Fernando,
Y mueran los tiranos!

BARRILDO.
Your turn, Frondoso.

FRONDOSO.
                    Here we go.
Anyone who doesn't like it,
Will he please keep his mouth shut.

(*Singing*) To Isabel I sing,
And Ferdinand, her King,
Who love and rule as one.
On the day that they are done,
God take them by the hand,
Unto the Promised Land.
Victory to our King and Queen,
And death to the abusers!

CITIZENS (*singing*).
Victory to our King and Queen,
Isabel y Fernando,
And death to the abusers!

LAURENCIA.
Barrildo, your turn.

BARRILDO.
                    I'm ready.
But singing is not my strong point.

PASCUALA.

> Take a deep breath, and sing it loud.
> We'll all clap and say you were great!

BARRILDO (*singing*).

> Here's to our Catholic Kings,
> Doing such wonderful things.
> Bringing justice to our land.
> They hold our future in their hands.
> Let's hope they always shall
> Defeat the King of Portugal.
> Victory to our King and Queen,
> And death to the abusers!

CITIZENS (*singing*).

> Victory to our King and Queen,
> *Isabel y Fernando,*
> And death to the abusers!

LAURENCIA.

> It's Mengo time!

FRONDOSO.

> Ready, Mengo?

MENGO.

> As a poet I'm but a novice.

PASCUALA.

> Though as a whipping post, your butt
> Has seen some action! Sing it.

MENGO (*singing*).

> One night my skin was torn,
> They left my bum forlorn.
> They beat it hard and made it sore,

Oh, it still drips with blood and gore.
Now Guzmán's gone, a pile of bone,
Bastard should have left my arse alone!
Victory to our King and Queen,
And death to the abusers!

CITIZENS (*singing*).
Victory to our King and Queen,
Isabel y Fernando,
And death to the abusers!
Muchos años vivan
Isabel y Fernando,
Y mueran los tiranos!

Enter ESTEBAN *and* JUAN ROJO, *carrying a new coat of arms.*

ESTEBAN.
Will someone take that figure down?

MENGO.
It's like a ghost haunting the square.

The head and the pole are removed.

ESTEBAN.
Here comes the new escutcheon.

FRONDOSO.
Show us our new coat of arms.

JUAN ROJO.
Where would you like me to display this?

ESTEBAN.
There. On the doors of the town hall.

LEONELO.
  It makes me proud.

BARRILDO.
                          It's beautiful.

FRONDOSO.
  Our dark times are almost over.
  The sun is beginning to rise.

ESTEBAN.
  Let us salute the proud colours
  Of Aragon and Old Castile.
  And may this town never again
  Live under tyranny's darkness.
  Now, Fuente Ovejuna, will you
  Listen to some words of advice?
  You know, I think it never hurts
  To pay attention to the old folk.
  What's happened here can't be ignored,
  There'll be an investigation.
  The King and Queen might get involved,
  We're on the route they're taking south.
  We must know what we're going to say.

FRONDOSO.
  What do you suggest?

ESTEBAN.
                          We stick together!
  And when the interrogator asks,
  We speak these words and nothing else:
  'Fuente Ovejuna did it.'

FRONDOSO.
  That's a good answer. And it's true.
  Fuente Ovejuna did it.

ESTEBAN.
Is everyone happy with this?

ALL.
                              We are.

ESTEBAN.
Now, let's rehearse what might happen
So we're ready when trouble comes.
I'll play the interrogator,
And you, Mengo, you'll play yourself
On the rack.

MENGO.
                    But shouldn't you use
Someone more likely to confess?

ESTEBAN.
But you're the best actor!

MENGO.
                              Let's do it.

ESTEBAN.
Peasant! Who killed the Commander?

MENGO.
Fuente Ovejuna did it.

ESTEBAN.
Rustic scum, you'll die on this rack.

MENGO.
Kill me! I am saying nothing.

ESTEBAN.
Criminal! Confess!

MENGO.

Stop! Enough!

ESTEBAN.
Who killed him?

MENGO.

Fuente Ovejuna!

ESTEBAN.
The people of Fuente Ovejuna
Shit on this investigation.

Enter ALONSO.

ALONSO.
Laughing? You haven't heard the news.

FRONDOSO.
Alonso, what's happened? Speak out.

ALONSO.
King Ferdinand has sent a judge.

ESTEBAN.
Everyone go directly home.

ALONSO.
He's come with a battalion of troops.

ESTEBAN.
Let him come with an army of devils!
We all know what we have to say.

ALONSO.
They're smashing down people's doors, and
Arresting children in the street.

ESTEBAN.
>   Friends, there's no need to be afraid.
>   Mengo, please, remind us all:
>   Who killed the Commander!

MENGO.
>   We did. Fuente Ovejuna.

Exit all.

Scene Six

The residence of the GRAND MASTER *of Calatrava, Almagro.*

Enter the GRAND MASTER *of Calatrava and* CIMBRANOS.

MASTER.
>   You're sure! This actually happened?
>   It's obscene! What a way to die!
>   And you, slave, deserve to die for
>   Bringing me such terrible news.

CIMBRANOS.
>   My lord, I am the messenger.
>   I have no desire to distress you.

MASTER.
>   The whole town rose against him?
>   Murdered him, and looted his home?
>   I'll visit this remote, lawless place
>   With five hundred troops and I will
>   Wipe it off the face of the earth!
>   No one will remember their names!

CIMBRANOS.
>   Sire, you must proceed with caution.

The people have sworn allegiance
To Ferdinand and Isabella;
Don't provoke the Catholic Kings.

MASTER.

How can they change their allegiance,
They are subjects of Calatrava?

CIMBRANOS.

You must negotiate that with
King Ferdinand, but it wouldn't be wise
To take military action.

MASTER.

If the town has pledged itself
To Ferdinand and Isabel
I'll never regain sovereignty.
My only course now is to accept
The victory of the Catholic Kings.
It's time to swallow my anger
And my pride and sue for peace.
Though I've grievously offended,
My youth is some kind of excuse,
I will go and beg forgiveness.
This is the true path and I will
Not shirk the way of honour.

Exit both.

Scene Seven

In the street, outside LAURENCIA's *front door, Fuente Ovejuna.*

Enter LAURENCIA.

LAURENCIA.
When danger threatens the lives of those we cherish
A new pain is added to the lover's sphere,
For fear generates a fresh and brutal anguish
When the peril that surrounds our loved ones is severe.
And even if our hearts are without blemish,
They are quickly swayed when overrun by fear,
It is hard to face the loss of all we relish,
And watch anxiety destroy all we hold most dear.
I love my husband: think only of his good
But to be sure of his survival he can't stay here,
That he is still alive is an act of God:
But how will I live without him always near?
He stays, my heart is torn with constant fears.
He goes, I cry a sea of bitter tears.

FRONDOSO.
Laurencia!

LAURENCIA.
        Frondoso. Husband.
This is reckless! You have to go!

FRONDOSO.
Concern for you brings me here,
Is 'Go away' my only welcome?!

LAURENCIA.
My love, I am thinking of you.
It's dangerous and I'm frightened.

FRONDOSO.

Dear Heaven, keep me from breeding
Fear in this brave woman's heart.

LAURENCIA.

You know all our neighbours have been
Arrested and are soon to be
Interrogated and tortured:
Don't you fear the judge's anger?
My love, try to avoid danger,
Not seek it out. Save your life! Run!

FRONDOSO.

Do you think I could run away?
Abandon my friends and family?
Stop seeing this beautiful face?
Stop looking into these beautiful eyes?
Never. Don't ask me. It's not right.
How could I live with myself if
To save my own selfish skin
I turned my back on all I cherish,
All that makes me who I am?

A cry, off.

I heard a cry.

LAURENCIA.

                    The interrogation.

JUDGE and PRISONERS speak, off.

LAURENCIA and FRONDOSO listen on stage.

JUDGE.

Speak, old fool, tell me the truth.

FRONDOSO.
>Laurencia, they're torturing
>An old man.

LAURENCIA.
>   Without mercy!

ESTEBAN.
>Enough, I've had enough!

JUDGE.
>   Release him!
>So, who killed Commander Guzmán?

ESTEBAN.
>Who? Fuente Ovejuna!

LAURENCIA.
>Father, your name will live for ever!

FRONDOSO.
>Esteban, you did it!

JUDGE.
>   Little boy.
>You know the name of the killer!
>Not going to speak? Pull harder there!
>Who killed Commander Guzmán?
>In the King's name, peasants, I swear
>I will kill you all with my bare hands:
>Boy, who killed Commander Guzmán?

BOY.
>Fuente Ovejuna did it.

FRONDOSO.
>They put a child on the rack
>And even he won't be broken.

LAURENCIA.
Our people are brave!

FRONDOSO.
                              Brave and strong!

JUDGE.
Bring the girl here, that one, quickly!
Tie her down and tighten the screws.
Pull that rope. Harder! Fool! Scum!

LAURENCIA.
He's blind with rage.

JUDGE.
                              Listen, woman!
I don't care if you die on this rack!
Tell me, who killed the Commander?

PASCUALA.
Fuente Ovejuna did it!

JUDGE.
Harder! Pull!

FRONDOSO.
                              He's wasting his time!

LAURENCIA.
That's Pascuala. She's being so strong!

FRONDOSO.
How can you be surprised when
Even the children won't confess!

JUDGE.
Tighter there!

PASCUALA.

          God in Heaven, help me!

JUDGE.

    Tighter! Tighter! Give me a name!

PASCUALA.

    Fuente Ovejuna!

JUDGE.

          Get rid of her!
    Bring me the fat peasant. Yes! Him!
    That's right. Rip the shirt off his back!

LAURENCIA.

    Now it's Mengo's turn to be brave.

FRONDOSO.

    I'm afraid that Mengo might break.

MENGO.

                    Ah!

JUDGE.

    Will you tighten those screws!

MENGO.

              Ah! Ah!

JUDGE.

    You there! Help him. Pull!

MENGO.

             Ah! Ah! Ah!

JUDGE.

    So, now, are you ready to speak?
    Who killed the Commander? Tell me!

MENGO.
  I'll speak, I'll speak, I'll tell you who.

JUDGE.
  You, put some slack in that rope there.

FRONDOSO.
  He's broken. He's going to speak.

JUDGE.
  Now, do you want another stretch?
  Or are you ready to confess?

MENGO.
  I've had enough pain, I'll confess.

JUDGE.
  So, who killed Commander Guzmán?

MENGO (*laughing*).
  The folk who dig fields and tend sheep!
  Fuente Ovejuna! We did it!

JUDGE.
  A conspiracy of rogues and cheats
  Who laugh in the face of torture!
  The man I most expected to break
  Offered the greatest resistance:
  Untie his hands. I'm tired of this.

FRONDOSO.
  May Heaven bless you, Mengo.
  I feared you'd break but your courage
  Proved much stronger than my faith.

  Enter the CITIZENS *of Fuente Ovejuna.*

BARRILDO.
  Mengo! You did it!

FRONDOSO.
                    You didn't break!

BARRILDO.
  Mengo! You're a hero!

FRONDOSO.
                    You did it!

MENGO.
  Ah. Ah.

BARRILDO.
            Take this, my friend, and drink.
  Something to eat?

MENGO.
                    What?

BARRILDO.
                              Rice pudding.

MENGO.
  Uh! Uh.

FRONDOSO.
            Have some wine.

BARRILDO.
                              There we go.

FRONDOSO.
  He's gulping that down, he'll live.

LAURENCIA.
  You must give him something to eat.

MENGO.
  Uh. Uh.

BARRILDO.
          Empty this bottle for me.

LAURENCIA.
  Nothing wrong with his throat it seems.

FRONDOSO.
  Being tortured is thirsty work.

BARRILDO.
  Another bottle?

MENGO.
            Ah! Ah! Ah!

FRONDOSO.
  Drink. You deserve every mouthful!

LAURENCIA.
  A glug for every turn of the screw.

FRONDOSO.
  Cover his shoulders, he's shaking.

BARRILDO.
  More?

MENGO.
        Yes! More! Another bottle!

FRONDOSO.
  I think he'd like some more.

BARRILDO.
  Mengo, down as much as you like.
  The hero of the rack can drink
  As much as he needs. What's wrong?

MENGO.
> Tastes like vinegar. Oh, oh dear.
> Take me in, I'm feeling shaky.

FRONDOSO.
> Take him in. Put him to bed. And
> Mengo, who killed the Commander?

MENGO.
> Peasant louts and drunken shepherds.
> Fuente Ovejuna. We did it.

Exit all but FRONDOSO *and* LAURENCIA.

FRONDOSO.
> And now, my love, tell me the truth:
> Who killed Commander Guzmán?

LAURENCIA.
> Fuente Ovejuna.

FRONDOSO.
> You can tell me:
> Who actually killed him?

LAURENCIA.
> I told you!
> Fuente Ovejuna!

FRONDOSO.
> And you:
> How did I ever conquer you?

LAURENCIA.
> With love, with loving me so much.

Exit both.

Scene Eight

Córdoba.

Enter FERDINAND *and* ISABELLA.

ISABELLA.
　My lord, I'm surprised and pleased
　To see you here in Córdoba.

FERDINAND.
　The joy of seeing you, my lady,
　Brings new light to my eyes.
　I was on my way to Portugal
　And couldn't resist a detour.

ISABELLA.
　I hope, my lord, you will
　Never resist such diversions.

FERDINAND.
　How did you leave Castile?

ISABELLA.

　　　　　　　　　　At peace.
　Order and unity restored.

FERDINAND.
　I'm pleased but not surprised, my lady,
　As you've worked so hard for peace.

Enter DON MANRIQUE.

MANRIQUE.
　The Master of Calatrava
　Is outside and requests an
　Audience with Your Majesties.

ISABELLA.

    I've looked forward to this meeting.

MANRIQUE.

    I would ask you to remember
    That though he is young and reckless
    He is a courageous soldier.

Enter the GRAND MASTER *of Calatrava.*

MASTER.

    Don Rodrigo Téllez Girón,
    Grand Master of Calatrava,
    Comes here in all humility
    To beg forgiveness for the wrong,
    The very great wrong, he's done you.
    I gave heed to the bad advice
    Of Fernán Gómez de Guzmán,
    Who spoke to my vanity and pride,
    False councillors both, and now
    On my knees I ask your pardon:
    If you consider me worthy
    Of mercy, a mercy I withheld
    From others, I will happily
    Pledge my life to your service,
    Giving all that I have to support
    Your campaign in Granada,
    Where I will show my true worth
    Wielding this sword in your cause,
    Putting your enemies to flight,
    Hanging red-crossed banners from
    The highest battlements of the Moor.
    I place at your disposal
    An army of five hundred men,

And I promise never again
To cause you anger or distress.

FERDINAND.
Rise, young Master, from the ground.
Such sincerity will always
Find a welcome in these arms.

MASTER.
You bring comfort to the penitent.

ISABELLA.
You have shown grace and wisdom
In all your words and actions here.

MASTER.
My lady, as beautiful as Esther.
My lord, as merciful as Xerxes.

MANRIQUE.
Your Majesty, the magistrate
You sent to Fuente Ovejuna
Has returned and wishes to present
His report: will you receive him?

FERDINAND.
Will you judge these assassins?

MASTER.
Were it in my power, my lord,
I'd punish this town severely.
They murdered the High Commander
Of the Order of Calatrava.

FERDINAND.
That duty is no longer yours.

ISABELLA.

    Rodrigo, we'll hear the evidence,
    Make our judgement and then place
    Their punishment in your hands.

Enter JUDGE.

JUDGE.

    I visited, as you instructed,
    The town of Fuente Ovejuna
    And with due care and diligence
    Conducted an investigation:
    At the conclusion of which I
    Must report I've not managed to
    Record one word of evidence,
    Or, indeed, the name of a single
    Guilty party, as the people
    Of the town when asked, answered
    Every one of my enquiries
    With a fearless resilience:
    'Fuente Ovejuna did it.'
    I tortured three hundred souls
    With the utmost severity
    And can assure Your Majesties
    They would utter nothing else:
    Boys of ten were stretched on the rack
    Every kind of strategy from
    Brutality to flattery
    Was employed but to no avail.
    As it has proved impossible
    To gain any hard evidence,
    I believe you have two options:
    You must either pardon them all

Or you must execute them all.
They're outside and beg permission
To plead their case in person and
Give you a chance to question them.

FERDINAND.
We will hear their plea, let them in.

Enter the CITIZENS *of Fuente Ovejuna.*

ISABELLA.
Are these the brutal assassins?

ESTEBAN.
Your Majesty, before you kneels
Fuente Ovejuna: we come here
Today, in all humility:
Your loyal and faithful subjects.
The cruel tyranny of the late
Commander was the cause of
The devastation in our town.
He abused us and our property,
He terrorised our womenfolk.
He was a stranger to mercy.

FRONDOSO.
This woman, whom Heaven in its
Kindness has given to me as wife,
Making me the luckiest of men,
He snatched on our wedding day,
Made her a prisoner in his house.
She fought him like a lioness,
And were she not the strongest, most
Honourable of women, it's plain
What he would have done to her.

MENGO.

> I think it's time I said my piece.
> Great King, mighty Queen, I warn you
> The story I'm about to tell
> May surprise and even shock you:
> When I tried to keep this woman
> Out of the clutches of his men,
> Who were at that moment trying
> To abduct her, that man, who was
> As cruel and perverse as Nero,
> Gave orders that his soldiers should
> Treat me in a way that's left my
> Bottom looking exactly like
> Two slices of fresh-cut salmon.
> Three strong and muscular soldiers
> Set about my backside with such
> Violence, vigour and persistence,
> I fear the scars may never heal:
> In an attempt to make my buttocks
> Whole again I've purchased so many
> Oils, plasters, bandages and cream,
> I've been forced to sell most of my flock.

ESTEBAN.

> Your Majesty, we wish to live
> Under your jurisdiction: we
> Believe you're our true master.
> We have hung your coat of arms
> On the doors of our town hall.
> We appeal to your mercy.

FERDINAND.

> This was a terrible crime: but
> As there's no evidence to prove

Who is responsible, I believe
We've no choice but to pardon you.
And as you've sworn allegiance to us,
We will rule your town directly
Until a Commander can be found
Worthy to govern such a people.

FRONDOSO.

Your Majesties, we thank you
For your wisdom and mercy.

LAURENCIA.

And here, my respected friends,
Our play, *Fuente Ovejuna*, ends.

The End.